We hope you enjoy this book. Please return or renew it by the due date.

You can renew it at www.norfolk.gov.uk/libraries or by using our free library app.

Otherwise you can phone 0344 800 8020 - please have your library card and PIN ready.

You can sign up for email reminders too.

NmL /AFT

K
T

ng
ks

by
all

Contents

At-a-glance

Walk		Page	⬭	🏠	✕	⛰	🕐
1	Stanton Moor	10	Birchover	SK 236621	3 miles (4.8km)	470ft (145m)	1½ hrs
2	Grin Low and Buxton Country Park	12	Grin Low	SK 049719	4½ miles (7.2km)	620ft (190m)	2 hrs
3	Heights of Abraham and Bonsall	14	Matlock Bridge Park	SK 295602	4¼ miles (6.8km)	1,060ft (325m)	2 hrs
4	Hagg Side and Lockerbrook Heights	16	Fairholmes Nat. Park Centre	SK 172893	4½ miles (7.2km)	885ft (270m)	2½ hrs
5	Hope and Win Hill	18	Hope	SK 171835	4½ miles (7.2km)	1,055ft (320m)	2½ hrs
6	Longshaw and Padley Gorge	20	Longshaw Country Park	SK 266800	5 miles (8km)	840ft (255m)	2½ hrs
7	Stanage Edge	22	Upper Burbage Bridge	SK 260830	5½ miles (8.9km)	900ft (275m)	2½ hrs
8	Chelmorton to Deep Dale	24	Wye Dale	SK 103724	5¼ miles (8.4km)	810ft (245m)	2½ hrs
9	Chinley Head	28	Chinley	SK 040827	5½ miles (8.9km)	1,250ft (380m)	3 hrs
10	Ashford in the Water and Monsal Dale	31	Ashford in the Water	SK 194697	6 miles (9.7km)	1,130ft (345m)	3 hrs
11	Lyme Park	34	Lyme Park	SJ 963823	6 miles (9.7km)	1,000ft (305m)	3 hrs
12	Redmires Reservoirs	37	Wyming Brook	SK 268858	6 miles (9.7km)	850ft (260m)	3 hrs
13	Tissington and Alsop en le Dale	40	Tissington	SK 178520	6¼ miles (10.1km)	820ft (250m)	3 hrs
14	Digley Reservoir	43	Digley Reservoir	SE 109067	6¼ miles (10.1km)	1,075ft (330m)	3 hrs
15	Black Moss and Butterley Reservoir	46	Marsden	SE 047118	6¼ miles (10.1km)	1,080ft (330m)	3 hrs
16	Castleton and Mam Tor	49	Castleton	SK 149 829	6¼ miles (10.1km)	1,325ft (405m)	3 hrs
17	The Manifold Valley	52	Wetton	SK 109 551	6½ miles (10.5km)	1,420ft (435m)	3½ hrs
18	The Goyt Valley and Shining Tor	55	Errwood Reservoir	SK 012748	6½ miles (10.5km)	1,310ft (400m)	3½ hrs
19	Cromford and Matlock Bath	58	Cromford Wharf	SK 299570	7 miles (11.3km)	1,390ft (425m)	3½ hrs
20	A Five Dales Walk	61	Tideswell	SK 152757	6¾ miles (10.9km)	1,250ft (380m)	3½ hrs
21	Three Shire Heads and Axe Edge Moor	64	Cat and Fiddle Inn	SK 000718	7¼ miles (11.7km)	1,080ft (330m)	3½ hrs
22	Hathersage	67	Hathersage	SK 231813	7¼ miles (11.7km)	1,400ft (425m)	3½ hrs
23	Lantern Pike	71	Hayfield	SK 036869	7¼ miles (11.7km)	1,400ft (425m)	3½ hrs
24	Beresford and Wolfscote Dales	76	Hartington	SK 128604	8 miles (12.9km)	1,360ft (415m)	4 hrs
25	Macclesfield Forest and the 'Cheshire Matterhorn'	79	Wildboarclough	SJ 986699	7¾ miles (12.5km)	1,770ft (540m)	4 hrs
26	Derwent Edge	82	Fairholmes Nat. Park Centre	SK 172893	9 miles (14.5km)	1,600ft (490m)	4½ hrs
27	Edale and Jacob's Ladder	85	Edale	SK 123853	8 miles (12.9km)	1,690ft (515m)	4 hrs
28	Lathkill Dale	88	Monyash	SK 149666	10½ miles (16.9km)	1,600ft (490m)	5 hrs

Comments

Gritstone outcrops and prehistoric remains abound on Stanton Moor, competing for your attention with fine views over the Derwent Valley.

The walk centres on the pastures and woodlands of Buxton Country Park, leaving time to visit the area's great show cave, Poole's Cavern.

The Heights of Abraham, famed for its views across Matlock's Derwent Gorge, and an attractive village with market cross and pub are features here.

Hillside forest, lakeside and a short ridge highlight different aspects of the higher reaches of the Derwent Valley.

Win Hill is one of the few Peakland tops rising to a distinguished peak and, although demanding a stiff climb, enjoys a fine prospect.

Scenic and historic interest on this walk from the former hunting lodge of the Duke of Rutland abounds, but the undoubted highlight is the lovely Padley Gorge.

Stanage Edge is one of the finest escarpments of the north-eastern moors. Easily attained from Upper Burbage it offers a grand high-level walk.

The great beauty of the White Peak lies within its dales and Deep Dale is no exception with moss-draped woodland and steep wildflower meadows rising to rocky crags above.

After an initial pull through old quarries above the town, the route wanders the margin between farm and moorland around Chinley Head.

The superb viewpoint of Monsal Head serves as a dramatic prelude to this grand promenade of Monsal Dale and the River Wye.

Overlooking Manchester's suburbs from the edge of the National Park, the expanse of Lyme Park offers superb walking, extensive views and an opportunity to visit a grand mansion.

Once a training ground for the Sheffield Pals regiment, the lonely Redmires moors are now popular with walkers escaping the busyness of the nearby city.

A section of the Tissington Trail, a disused railway track that ran between Buxton and Ashbourne, here links two of the Peak's most picturesque villages.

Tucked beneath the foreboding mass of Black Hill, the third highest in the Peak, the picturesque village of Holme is visited on this moorland promenade from Digley Reservoir.

The deep valleys above Marsden rise to the watershed of England. This ramble climbs onto the moors for a glimpse of Lancashire before finding a scenic return route past the reservoirs of the Wessenden Valley.

The narrow confines of Cave Dale contrast with the superb airy ridge of Mam Tor on this satisfying walk from Castleton, which should still leave time to visit one of the famous caves.

Among the features here are the disused trackbed of the former Manifold railway line, an old corn mill and a gaping cave high on the hillside.

Shining Tor is the highest of the south Peak's hills, reached here along its northern ridge to reveal an unrivalled prospect over the Goyt Valley and surrounding countryside.

A Victorian spa, an early purpose-built town of the Industrial Revolution, a superb viewpoint and a picturesque canal are all featured in this day out from Cromford.

Five dales in a day, with every one different. The walk sets out from the lively village of Tideswell, whose grand church is known as the 'Cathedral of the Peak'.

From the remote Cat and Fiddle Inn, this wild and wonderful ramble encircles moorland heads of the White Peak's major rivers, following the Dane to a pretty waterfall known as Three Shire Heads.

Literature, legend and landscape come together in this ramble from Hathersage. Associations with Charlotte Brontë, Jane Eyre, Robin Hood and Little John are all in this beautiful Derwent countryside.

Beginning from the attractive town of Hayfield, this circuit skirts the outlying flanks of the Kinder plateau to return over the former beacon hill of Lantern Pike and along the course of an old railway.

The River Dove's succession of limestone gorges begins with Beresford and Wolfscote dales, which inspired Charles Cotton's contribution to his friend, Izaac Walton's fishing treatise, *The Compleat Angler*.

Distant views from the north reveal Shutlingsloe as a worthy 'Cheshire Matterhorn', a satisfying objective of this wandering circuit within the ancient royal hunting domain of Macclesfield Forest.

Overlooking the Derwent and Ladybower reservoirs, Derwent Edge is punctuated with extraordinary rock formations, thoroughly justifying it as one of the Dark Peak's classic walks.

This ramble combines a dramatic ascent along Grindsbrook Clough with a superb edge walk past some of the exciting formations that dot the rim of the Kinder plateau.

The open vistas of limestone plateau contrast with intimate scenes in the narrow gorge below on this day-long ramble through ever popular Lathkill Dale.

Keymap

WEST YORKSHIRE

Marsden **15**

Holmfirth

14 Scholes

Holme

Oldham

Barnsley

GREATER MANCHESTER

Ashton-under-Lyne

Manchester

Penistone

Stocksbridge

SOUTH YORKSHIRE

Bleaklow Hill

Glossop

Derwent Reservoir

Sheffield

Stockport

4 **26** Ladybower Reservoir

23 High Peak

Hayfield

27 Edale

12 Redmires Reservoirs

New Mills

Disley

11

9

Chinley

Castleton

16

5 Hope

22 Hathersage

7

Chapel-en-le-Frith

6 Nether Padley

Shining Tor

Errwood Reservoir

Tideswell

20

Baslow

Macclesfield

18 Buxton

2

8

10 DERBYSHIRE

Chesterfield

CHESHIRE

Macclesfield Canal

Shutlingsloe

Wildboarclough

25 **21**

Chelmorton

Bakewell

Monyash

28

Dane

Youlgrave

1

Congleton

Churnet

Leek

STAFFORDSHIRE

Caldon Canal

Dove

Hartington

24

17

Wetton

13 Tissington

Cromford

Matlock

3

19

Carsington Water

Ashbourne

Longdendale

Don

Dearne

Introduction to More Peak District

Well before its designation as Britain's first National Park in 1951, the Peak District had assumed iconic status for many who appreciated the freedom and beauty of open and unspoiled landscapes. This yearning was no hark-back to a Victorian idyllicism of nature, but was instead founded upon basic human desires for physical and mental rejuvenation. Set fairly between the growing industrial centres of Manchester, Sheffield, Stoke and Derby, the fresh countryside of the Peak offered a brief escape from the toil of workaday lives and its exploration by ordinary townsfolk inspired a tradition of rambling and climbing clubs. But the liberties were hard-won, for this was private land, and the area will forever be associated with the Kinder Trespass of 1932, an action that turned a tide of public sympathy and ultimately proved a fundamental step in establishing the countryside freedoms we enjoy today.

Viewed from the south, the Peak District is the first manifestation of the Pennine hills, a broad and often deserted rumpled uplift that continues all the way to the Scottish border, and which effectively divides the northern part of England, east from west. The hills erupt with a surprising suddenness from the surrounding lowlands as a lofty, but deeply cleft expanse of limestone, fringed east and west by long horns of gritstone that come together and extend far to the north beneath a shroud of peat bog and moss. The separation into White and Dark peaks reflects the disparate natures of the rock upon which each is rooted, although the simplistic north-south division suggested by the Ordnance Survey Explorer maps is upset by the arcs of gritstone bracketing the central limestone plateau of the southern sheet.

Early travellers marvelled poetically at the Peak's natural wonders; dark caverns, plummeting holes, sparkling trout-filled streams and health-giving mineral springs, but were equally awed by imagined horrors besetting the melancholy moors that lay beyond.

Above Ashway Rocks

Like the rest of the Pennines, the Peak District is nowhere overly high, but some of the wildest and seemingly remotest areas of England are to be found among its most elevated reaches. In dramatic contrast, the lower slopes and valley folds shelter picturesque villages that are set against a glorious backdrop that has been shaped by countless generations of diligent husbandry. This great diversity of landscapes within a relatively compact area bestows an especial charm upon the National Park, which, attracting more than 10 million people is the most visited in the country. Such popularity can bring congestion to its most famous beauty spots, yet there are many places to find solitude, even during a Bank Holiday weekend.

Dark Peak

The rugged gritstones of the Dark Peak are the uplifted consolidation of

Descending towards Goyt's Clough

sands, pebbles and muds deposited by a vast river system that drained a high landmass far to the north. In warmer, drier times, these rolling uplands supported woodlands and farming, but prehistoric clearance, overuse and a changing climate has left them an upland wilderness, relieved only by occasional eroded tors. Spike rush, cotton grass, heathers and bilberry intersperse wetter areas of peat bog, which have been eroded to create a bizarre landscape of groughs (deep troughs) and hags (black islands of peat). A wild beauty is revealed through the changing seasons with the new greens of spring, the rich purple of flowering heather, the subtle hues of autumn or the pristine blanket of winter snow.

Drama comes around the fringes where the high ground falls into deep valleys or finishes in abrupt and fantastically weatherworn escarpments and cliffs. Locally they are aptly referred to as 'edges' and the challenge of their intricate faces attracts climbers from around the world. The most sensational of these parallels the eastern boundary of the park and runs for over 12 miles (19km) in a succession of breathtaking views. Over the centuries, the rock has proved an admirable material for building and the faces of disused quarries sometimes blend with the line of natural cliffs. In places, the stone was worked on an industrial scale to build the surrounding towns, providing not only ashlar blocks, but also paving stones and roofing slabs as well as cisterns and troughs. Elsewhere, the rock was suited for the production of millstones, which the National Park has

The heath above the head of Black Brook

adopted as its symbol.

Although there are no natural lakes within the Peak District, there is an abundance of reservoirs, which were constructed from the middle of the 19th century onwards to satisfy the ever-increasing demands of urbanisation and industrialisation. Several of these are featured among these walks, and though the lost beauty of the valleys that were drowned might be regretted, most have settled within their landscape to project a different attractiveness upon the landscape.

White Peak
Underlying it all, but laid bare in the southern part of the National Park, is Carboniferous limestone, the accumulation of corals and shells in a shallow tropical sea that covered much of what is now England some 350 million years ago. In many places you can spot fossils embedded in the rock, a common find being the segmented stems of crinoids, an ancient animal that survives today as the sea lily. Karst scenery brings its own geological wonders in disappearing and resurgent streams, dry valleys and dark caves. Small caves are to be found in many of the valleys, but the most dramatic are the show caves at Castleton and Buxton. However, not all the holes in the ground are natural and mining for lead and copper were widespread activities from at least Roman times until the beginning of the 20th century. The Romans also mined the semi-precious Blue John fluorite at Castleton, a practice that continues today, although the amounts taken are small and used for jewellery.

Like the gritstone farther north, the limestone was extensively quarried and used for building, and the rough-stone cottages and miles of stone walls are a distinctive feature of the area. More important was its conversion to lime, which was used as a fertiliser, for mortar and smelting of iron, and huge roasting kilns beside vast quarries disgorged lime into waiting railway wagons for transport out along the narrow winding valleys. Quarrying remains an important industry around Buxton, hence its exclusion from the National Park.

The upland pastures are devoted to grazing and, although often revealing far-reaching views, much of the White Peak's appeal derives from the deep gorges cleaving the high plateau. Streams, tangled woodlands and lush grazing in occasional water meadows contrast with dry valleys and flower-rich pastures where the water now flows deep underground. Each dale's unique character is reflected in its plant and wildlife and, as many are accessible only on foot, is delightful to discover.

Walking in the Peak

In exploring the area, the routes largely follow discernible paths, which in fine weather should present no great difficulty. However, if new to country walking, it is sensible to begin with the shorter walks, progressing as fitness and experience in finding your way about the countryside develops. The uplands of the Dark Peak can be intimidating and the longer rambles there demand a level of hill-walking experience. Within the White Peak, few places are remote from habitation or a lane, but as much of the land is actively farmed, it is important to stick to recognised paths. Be aware too that limestone and steep grass slopes can become very slippery, particularly when wet.

The track back across the fields, Tissington

This book includes a list of waypoints alongside the description of the walk, so that you can enjoy the full benefits of gps should you wish to. For more information about route navigation, improving your map reading ability, walking with a GPS and for an introduction to basic map and compass techniques, read Pathfinder® Guide *Navigation Skills for Walkers* by outdoor writer Terry Marsh (ISBN 978-0-319-09175-3). This title is available in bookshops and online at os.uk/shop

Stanage Edge

Stanton Moor

		GPS waypoints
Start	Birchover, by The Druid Inn	 SK 236 621
Distance	3 miles (4.8km)	Ⓐ SK 241 628
Height gain	470 feet (145m)	Ⓑ SK 249 635
Approximate time	1½ hours	Ⓒ SK 246 625
Parking	Roadside parking in Lower Village or parking area opposite Birchover Quarry on Birchover Road	Ⓓ SK 244 622
Route terrain	Heath and field paths	
Ordnance Survey maps	Landranger 119 (Buxton & Matlock), Explorer OL24 (The Peak District – White Peak area)	

Stanton Moor, a finger of gritstone amid limestone country, rises to 1,060 feet (323m) and is an open, breezy, heather-clad moorland giving glorious views across the valley of the Derwent. Its two chief characteristics, which form the main features of this short walk, are the curious rock formations and the vast number of prehistoric remains – burial chambers, standing stones, circles and fortifications – that litter the moor.

Birchover is a small village strung out along the hill that climbs to Stanton Moor. At its lower end, behind **The Druid Inn**, a path leads to the Rowtor Rocks, a gritstone outcrop worth exploring after the walk, both for its extensive views and its maze of caves and passages, where carved steps lead to staggered terraces. Many of these were the work of Thomas Eyre, an eccentric 18th-century clergyman, who also built, just beneath the rocks, the tiny village church.

🅿 The walk begins through a broad gap in the wall opposite **The Druid Inn**. A path climbs away between the trees, passing old quarries to emerge in a parking area at the top.

Walk through to the road beyond and turn left. Follow it up the hill for ¼ mile (400m), passing Birchover Quarry to find a marked footpath leaving on the right onto Stanton Moor Ⓐ.

Head through the trees to a stile and

Thomas Eyre's sanctuary

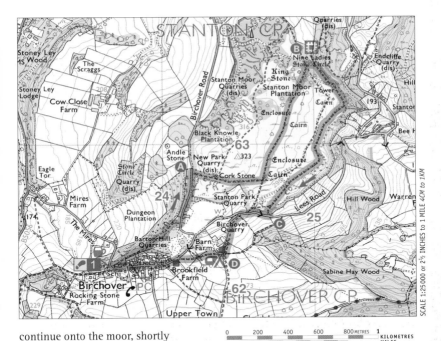

continue onto the moor, shortly reaching the Cork Stone, an isolated monolith on your left by a disused quarry. Bear right at the fork and keep going until you meet an obvious crossing of broad paths. Turn left and climb over open heather heath, where there are some fine views to the right across the Derwent Valley. After passing into birch woodland, look for the Nine Ladies Stone Circle in a clearing to the left, the most imposing of the many prehistoric remains that dot the moor. According to legend the ladies were turned to stone as punishment for dancing on the Sabbath. However, more prosaically the monument is thought to date from the Bronze Age and was probably erected around 1500BC. Like all such circles, nothing is really known about it, although it is presumed to have had some religious significance.

Walk a few yards beyond the circle and take a path off to the right **B**, following it through trees to a stile. Over that, turn right beside the fence above a steep escarpment, shortly passing the Reform Tower, erected in honour of Earl Grey, of Reform Bill (and blend of tea) fame. A little farther on, the path leads to a curious outcrop dubbed the Cat Stone, immediately before which, the path abruptly swings right. Keep going at the edge of the moor, passing more outcrops and eventually dropping to meet a lane **C**.

Turn right, but after some 200 yards, abandon the lane for a waymarked footpath on the left. Carry on beside a camping field to a farm at the bottom. Keep left past the yard and buildings to pick up a grass track off right signed to Winster. Pass through a gate at the end of the buildings, turning right immediately beyond over a squeeze stile **D**. Walk on by a fence to join a track from the farm that leads out to a lane. Follow it left downhill into the village, passing Birchover's other pub, **The Red Lion**, before returning to The Druid Inn. ●

Grin Low and Buxton Country Park

		GPS waypoints
Start	Grin Low and Buxton Country Park	⬈ SK 049 719
Distance	4½ miles (7.2km)	Ⓐ SK 054 717
Height gain	620 feet (190m)	Ⓑ SK 050 724
Approximate time	2 hours	Ⓒ SK 055 725
Parking	Car park at start (Honesty box)	Ⓓ SK 058 712
Route terrain	Farm tracks, field and woodland paths	Ⓔ SK 043 718
Ordnance Survey maps	Landranger 119 (Buxton & Matlock), Explorer OL24 (The Peak District – White Peak area)	

Buxton Country Park is centred on Grin Low Woods, a landscape once blighted by quarrying and lime burning. The short ramble takes in Solomon's Temple, a 19th-century folly and fine viewpoint and continues across the neighbouring hills, but allows plenty of time to visit the impressive show cave of Poole's Cavern.

Buxton is the Peak District's answer to Bath or Cheltenham – an elegant spa town with some fine buildings. Most notable are the 18th-century Crescent, the Devonshire Hospital, the Regency church, the Victorian Pavilion and gardens and the opulent Edwardian Opera House.

⬈ From the car park, a well-surfaced path signed to Poole's Cavern and Solomon's Temple climbs from the quarry. Meeting another path go left and then, at a second junction swing right through a gate. Walk on, initially beside Grin Low Woods before striking out to the folly, which breaks the skyline ahead Ⓐ. Solomon's Temple, otherwise known as Grinlow Tower, was built in 1896 by Solomon Mycock to provide work for the unemployed. From the top you can look out to Mam Tor and Kinder Scout. Heading north towards the town, mount a wall stile

and continue down to a broken wall. Go left, crossing a stile beside a gate into Grin Low Woods, which were planted by the sixth Duke of Devonshire in 1820 to hide the devastation of old lime pits. Walk ahead through the trees, ignoring side paths until you reach an obvious T-junction. To the right, the way

Looking from Stanley Moor to Grin Low

descends the hillside, eventually reaching a stepped path that drops right to Poole's Cavern car park **B**. An impressive natural cave, it yielded Roman artefacts and takes its name from a medieval outlaw who reputedly used it as his lair.

Cross the car park to a gate opposite from which a path leads past a cottage to the road. Walk right for ¼ mile (400m) before turning off right opposite College Road **C** along an enclosed track. Narrowing to a path, it continues through trees to emerge onto open grass. Carry on beside the right-hand edge, meeting a rough lane in front of houses. Walk right, but after a cattle-grid, leave right to pass through a wall gap. Turn left on a contained path towards Fern House Farm, mounting a stile and continuing past successive paddocks. Reaching the stables, dogleg around an equestrian exercise enclosure

to a yard, leaving beyond it along a rising track at the edge of a wood. Entering a field at the top, carry on to a stile and then by a wall to a second stile in the corner. Head downhill, bearing right from the wall through another gate. Over a crossing track, drop to leave the bottom corner onto Grin Low Road **D**.

Go left and then leave right, crossing a stile beside a gate to follow a track over a stream before winding uphill to a farm. Entering the yard, turn immediately right through a gate. Skirt the buildings to emerge onto a track. Heading from the farm, it meanders across the valley and later below the disued Stanley Moor Reservoir, offering superb views to Axe Edge.

Reaching the road **E**, cross to the country park and follow the drive back to the car park. The open ground has been reclaimed from old workings, whilst the main quarry was converted into an attractive campsite for the Caravan Club of Great Britain in 1981–2. ●

0	200	400	600	800 METRES	1	
0	200	400	600 YARDS	½		KILOMETRES MILES

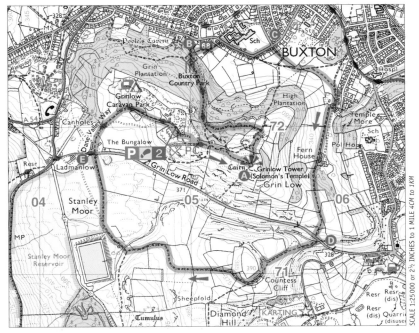

SCALE 1:25000 or 2½ INCHES to 1 MILE 4CM to 1KM

Heights of Abraham and Bonsall

		GPS waypoints
Start	Matlock Bridge Park	 SK 295 602
Distance	4¼ miles (6.8km)	Ⓐ SK 294 599
Height gain	1,060 feet (325m)	Ⓑ SK 293 592
Approximate time	2 hours	Ⓒ SK 291 587
Parking	Long stay car park on Derwent Way	Ⓓ SK 279 583
		Ⓔ SK 279 590
Route terrain	Woodland and field paths and tracks	
Ordnance Survey maps	Landranger 119 (Buxton & Matlock), Explorer OL24 (The Peak District – White Peak area)	

Beginning from Matlock Bridge, upstream of the spa, the walk climbs from the gorge to the former lead-mining village of Bonsall. The return follows old tracks across the high ground, which peers up the Derwent Valley towards the Chatsworth lands.

Leaving the riverside car park, turn right along the main road to the traffic lights. Go right and keep right up Snitterton Road. After 100 yards branch left on a track to Bridge Farm. Walk past the front of the farmhouse to the field behind and climb to a squeeze stile at the top Ⓐ. Follow a track left towards Matlock Bath, but approaching a bend before Greenhills Farm, leave

beside a gate on the left from which a twisting grass path undulates across hillside meadow. Entering woodland continue below Shining Cliff. Later meeting a narrow track, head up the hill. At the top look for a path on the right signed to the Heights of Abraham Ⓑ. Climb steeply beside a wall, passing through a gap before emerging from woodland onto a more open hillside. A superb view opens across the valley to the Victorian gothic Riber Castle and the cliffs below High Tor.

A trod guides you across the hillside then turns once more to face the gradient, rising through scrub towards a round tower, the Heights of Abraham. Reaching a side entrance to the complex Ⓒ, ignore the gate and follow the wall up to a collapsed stile. Walk above the boundary, crossing the main

Bonsall's market square and cross

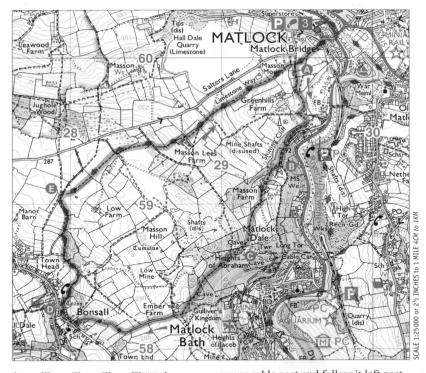

```
0    200   400   600   800 METRES   1
                                      KILOMETRES
                                      MILES
0    200   400   600 YARDS           ½
```

entrance drive and continue through woodland beyond.

Emerging from the trees onto a rough field track, go right through a gate and turn left to follow a track from Ember Farm. After cresting the hill, it winds down between leafy walls to Bonsall, ending opposite St James Church. Go right, but then branch right along a narrow alleyway to emerge above the square, dominated by a stepped market cross **D**.

Turn right along a restricted byway that climbs determinedly from the village. At a fork, go left, beyond which the gradient eases. Reaching another junction turn right for another short climb, looking for a dilapidated signpost and broken stile on the right near the crest of the hill **E**.

Head across to the end of a wall by a power cable post and follow it left past a barn. Continue across the next field to a track. Through a stile opposite, cut right to another stile and go left on the other flank of the wall, which guides you down a scrubby hillside to a kissing-gate. Passing out onto a track, walk right, but then leave after a few yards by a signpost on the left. Head down the edge of the field and across a smaller paddock to come out by the entrance to Masson Lees Farm. Opposite, the ongoing path descends more fields, shortly encountering a field track beneath overhead power cables. Slip through a gate and carry on down the hill with the hedge on your right. A trod guides you across successive enclosures, eventually reaching a wooden stile beyond which the path forks. Choose the right branch through scrub to emerge onto a track at Point **A**. The way back lies along your outward path through the stile opposite. ●

Hagg Side and Lockerbrook Heights

Hagg Side and Lockerbrook Heights

		GPS waypoints
Start	Fairholmes National Park Centre	
Distance	4½ miles (7.2km)	🖉 SK 172 893
Height gain	885 feet (270m)	Ⓐ SK 180 885
		Ⓑ SK 170 885
Approximate time	2½ hours	Ⓒ SK 164 891
Parking	At start – (Pay and Display)	Ⓓ SK 166 910
		Ⓔ SK 170 897
Route terrain	Forest tracks	
Ordnance Survey maps	Landranger 110 (Sheffield & Huddersfield), Explorer OL1 (The Peak District – Dark Peak area)	

After an initial stretch beside Ladybower, the route climbs the steep, forested flanks of Hagg Side to swing north across Lockerbrook Heights. There are views across Ashop, Edale and into the upper Derwent before dropping to an easy finish beside the Derwent reservoir and dam.

Despite the sense of natural beauty pervading the upper Derwent Valley, the scenescape is almost entirely due to man. The three vast lakes of Howden, Derwent and Ladybower were created as reservoirs to supply growing industrial cities and the conifer forests were planted for timber and to purify the water draining the catchment. Together with the open moorland of the upper slopes, the area annually attracts over two million visitors who explore the many pathways and tracks on foot or by bike, fish the lakes or simply admire the view.

The Derwent Dam

The woodlands around the visitor centre attract many small birds and in the clearings of the wider forest you might spot a goshawk hunting for a meal. Now becoming more common, these are bold hunters and will pursue other birds into the tree cover or take small mammals such as squirrels and rabbits.

🖉 From the **Fairholmes Visitor Centre**, go back to the road. Turn left and walk for ¼ mile (400m) to a roadside parking area from which you will find a path signed to the Bridge End car park. Dropping through the woodland fringe below the road, it undulates easily above the lake. Shortly after leaving the trees by a small, stone water-board building, bear right back to the road and cross to the Bridge End car park opposite Ⓐ. A broad loggers' track leaves beside it, climbing steeply into the plantation above. After some ½ mile (800m), the way rises more easily, shortly swinging left to end at a couple of gates and stiles Ⓑ. Through the right-hand gate, go right along an open track, once the old pack road across the moors to Glossop and which is signed to Alport Bridge. The Hagg Side plantation precludes a view to the lake far below, but over to the left the eye is drawn across the Ashop Valley to the bleak eastern promontory of the Kinder plateau. Farther back, overlooking Edale is the long ridge running from Lose Hill past the precipice of Back Tor to the distant Iron Age fortress of Mam Tor. Keep going above the edge of the forest, eventually crossing a stile beside a gate.

Drop to a meeting of tracks beyond **C**, and follow that to the right, heading almost due north. It carries on gradually downward beside the forest, eventually crossing Locker Brook to reach Lockerbrook Farm, now operating as an outdoors activity centre. Remain on the rising track through a gate beyond the farm, which soon crests to a long descent back in the trees. Ignore paths signed off to Fairholmes, continuing ever more steeply down until you ultimately reach the road at the foot of Ouzelden Clough **D**.

Follow the lakeside road to the right, eventually passing the Derwent Dam. The pilots of 617 Squadron used the valley during the spring of 1943 while training for a daring attack upon the Möhne, Eder and Sorpe dams in the industrial heartland of Nazi Germany. The reservoir was subsequently used as a location during the making of the 1955 film *The Dam Busters*. Nearby is a memorial to a faithful sheepdog, 'Tip', who guarded the body of her master for 15 weeks after he died on the Howden moors during the winter of 1953–54.

A few yards beyond, look for a path signed off from the parking area **E**, which drops into trees above the reservoir outflow. Keep left at a fork, and walk down steps out to another lane. Go right and almost immediately left on a path that leads back to the visitor centre and car park. ●

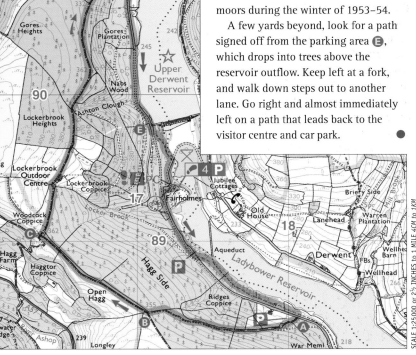

SCALE 1:25000 or 2½ INCHES to 1 MILE 4CM to 1KM

Hope and Win Hill

		GPS waypoints
Start	Hope	🥾 SK 171 835
Distance	4½ miles (7.2km)	Ⓐ SK 171 838
Height gain	1,055 feet (320m)	Ⓑ SK 186 850
Approximate time	2½ hours	Ⓒ SK 192 850
Parking	Car park on main street – Pay and Display	Ⓓ SK 186 839
		Ⓔ SK 179 837
Route terrain	Field and moorland paths	
Ordnance Survey maps	Landranger 110 (Sheffield & Huddersfield), Explorer OL1 (The Peak District – Dark Peak area)	

Although short, this walk involves a strenuous ascent of Win Hill, but the effort expended is amply rewarded with a panoramic view from the top. The enjoyable return through woodland, heath and field ends along the banks of the River Noe in the Hope Valley.

🥾 Go right out of the car park along the main street to the church and turn left into Edale Road. Stride up the lane for ¼ mile (400m) to a fork just after the school Ⓐ. Bear right along Bowden Lane signed to Hope Cemetery, the way dropping over the River Noe at Killhill Bridge. Climbing beyond, pass beneath a railway bridge and then turn right, the lane becoming a farm track as it curves away from the woodland bordering the line. Carry on up the hill to Twitchill Farm, walking through the yard to a gate at the top.

A path rises steeply ahead up the fellside to another gate, continuing in the next field to a stile at the top corner. A clear path carries on steadily upwards through the gorse, heather and bracken of open moorland, but pause occasionally to appreciate the views opening behind as you gain height. Beyond a broken wall, the gradient eases and the distinctive rocky peak of Win Hill now appears ahead. The main path makes straight for it, passing through a

kissing-gate to join another path for the final stretch to the summit Ⓑ.

To the north, the ground falls abruptly to the Ladybower Reservoir and above the timber-clad slopes of the Derwent Valley is the impressive line of Derwent Edge. Farther west is the brooding mass of Kinder Scout, while more immediately, across the head of the Hope Valley is Lose Hill, whose long ridge stretches back to Mam Tor and Lord's Seat.

The path follows the short but splendidly ragged ridge, the high point of the walk in more ways than one. From the end it falls quickly to a gate and, where the path forks beyond, take the left branch, into the Winhill Plantation. Continue down through the trees, in a little while reaching a junction of paths in front of a wall and fence Ⓒ.

To the right the way is signed to Thornhill and contours beside a wall around the hill. After some ¼ mile (400m), bear right at a junction through

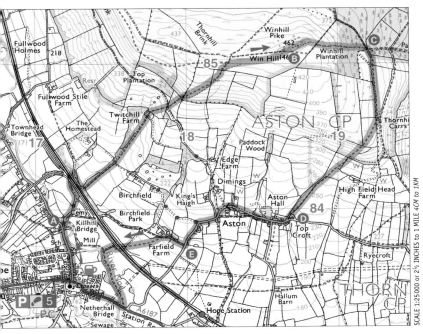

a gap in the wall. A lesser but still distinct path signed to Aston rises over a shoulder of bilberry and heather moor before losing height to a wall stile. Carry on down the hill, passing through a gate in the corner to continue along a narrow enclosure. Over a stile at the bottom follow a contained path, which leads onto a narrow lane **D**.

Turn right and keep with the main lane for a little over ¹⁄₂ mile (800m) past the old hall and scattered farms and

The trig point on Winhill Pike

cottages that comprise the hamlet of Aston. Despite the tarmac, the walking here is a delight, for the way drops below occasional wooded banks, the rocks oozing moisture and dripping with mosses and fern. Carry on until you reach a track off right to Farfield Farm **E**.

Follow it as far as the farmhouse and there bear off left on a track signed to the camping field that drops to a gate beside a barn. Leave through a small kissing-gate on the left and head away, initially beside the right-hand hedge and continuing beyond its end to a gate at the bottom of the field. Entering woodland bordering a railway embankment, go right and then left beneath a bridge into the field on the other side. Strike across to meet the bank of the River Noe and walk downstream alongside it to a bridge. Climb out to the main road and follow it across the river back into Hope. ●

Longshaw and Padley Gorge

		GPS waypoints
Start	Longshaw Country Park	
Distance	5 miles (8km)	🖉 SK 266 800
Height gain	840 feet (255m)	Ⓐ SK 268 789
Approximate time	2½ hours	Ⓑ SK 259 781
Parking	National Trust car park at start (Pay and Display)	Ⓒ SK 251 787
		Ⓓ SK 246 789
Route terrain	Moorland tracks, woodland paths	Ⓔ SK 257 800
Ordnance Survey maps	Landrangers 110 (Sheffield & Huddersfield) and 119 (Buxton & Matlock), Explorers OL24 (The Peak District – White Peak area) and OL1 (The Peak District – Dark Peak area)	

Open park, moor, dense woodland and a beautiful gorge lend great scenic variety to this walk. Add the historic interest of a 19th-century hunting lodge and a chapel wrought from a 14th-century manor and the result is a splendidly absorbing ramble.

🖉 From the bottom of the car park take the path down towards the visitor centre. After crossing a stream, turn left onto a track winding behind Longshaw Lodge signed to Wooden Pole Car Park. Now owned by the National Trust, Longshaw Country Park formed part of the Rutland estates, which were broken up in 1927. The palatial house was built a century earlier as a shooting lodge and after the sale was used as a guesthouse before being divided into private flats. Continue through the trees and then along a grass path, which runs at the foot of a low gritstone edge overlooking open parkland. Where it later splits, bear left, climbing to a road beside a junction.

Walk ahead, crossing the road from the right to a track leaving through a white-painted gate onto White Edge Moor Ⓐ. After passing the isolated White Edge Lodge, the way narrows to a grassy path that gradually loses height across the open moor. Bear left at a fork and continue down to meet the main road Ⓑ. Go left but almost at once cross and double back right through a gate returning into the Longshaw Estate. After ¼ mile (400m), as the track meets a plantation of larch and pine, drop over a stile on the left and follow a gently descending path across bracken moorland. Approaching Oak's Wood, the way falls to the head of a wooded gorge. Ignore a crossing path and bear right on a path that loses height beside a lively stream cascading steeply through the trees. Approaching the bottom, keep left where the path splits, dropping to the road near a cottage Ⓒ.

A few yards to the left a path leaves sharp right, falling abruptly to Grindleford Station. Go right, crossing first the railway as it emerges from the 3½-mile (5.6km) Totley Tunnel and then bending over Burbage Brook by Padley Mill. Stay ahead past a junction, following the track a little farther to Padley Chapel, Ⓓ just beyond a row of houses.

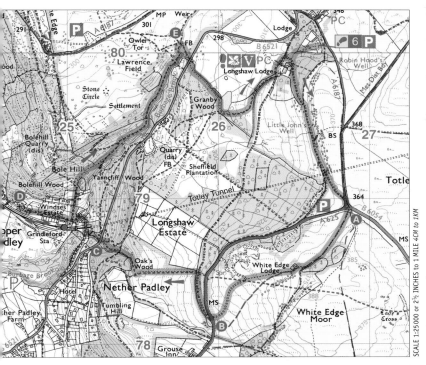

SCALE 1:25000 or 2½ INCHES to 1 MILE 4CM to 1KM

| 0 | 200 | 400 | 600 | 800 METRES | 1 |
| 0 | 200 | 400 | 600 YARDS | ½ |

KILOMETRES
MILES

Sir Thomas Fitzherbert's 14th-century house fell into ruins and only the gate-house survives, which was converted into a chapel in 1933.

Return past the houses to the junction and go left, climbing to the top of the track where a gate takes the way into Padley Gorge, one of the few remnants of ancient woodland surviving in the Peak District. The gradient later eases and the onward path undulates above Burbage Brook, which tumbles cheerily over the rocks in a succession of miniature waterfalls. Emerging quite suddenly into open heath, there is a superb view ahead to the escarpment of Burbage Rocks. Carry on beside the stream to find a bridge **E**. Cross and climb right to the road above. Through a gate diagonally opposite, follow a path rising beside Granby Wood. After skirting a pond the way shortly breaks to more open ground, following a line of rhododendron bushes to a junction of paths in a clump of yew. Go through the left gate, passing below the front of the lodge to meet the main drive. Walk left, right and then left again back to the car park. ●

Padley Chapel

Stanage Edge

			GPS waypoints
Start	Upper Burbage Bridge		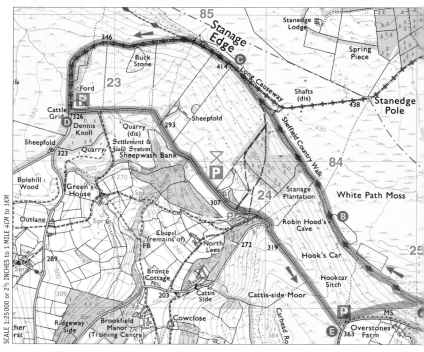 SK 260 830
Distance	5½ miles (8.9km)		Ⓐ SK 250 830
Height gain	900 feet (275m)		Ⓑ SK 244 835
Approximate time	2½ hours		Ⓒ SK 238 845
Parking	Car park west of bridge		Ⓓ SK 227 843
Route terrain	Clear moorland paths, rugged track and lane		Ⓔ SK 244 829
Ordnance Survey maps	Landranger 110 (Sheffield & Huddersfield), Explorer OL1 (The Peak District – Dark Peak area)		

Meaning simply 'Stone Edge', Stanage is part of the long gritstone escarpment bounding the eastern rim of the Derwent Valley. Easily attained, this superb, high-level stroll is full of dramatic interest every step of the way, descending an ancient highway to return along quiet country lanes.

Leaving the car park, follow the roadside verge left to a sharp bend, where a path strikes ahead across the

moor towards the southern abutment of Stanage Edge, some ¼ mile (400m) away. Approaching the rocky defences, the Cowper Stone becomes prominent to the right, a huge, detached boulder of gritstone, which offers a challenge to the most experienced rock climbers. Just about every nook and cranny along Stanage's 4-mile (6.4km) length offers a route to the top, encompassing all levels of difficulty from a simple scramble to extremely severe. Although barely 100 feet (30m) high, it embodies Britain's longest climbing route, a complete end-to-end traverse. There is nothing so demanding on this walk and the route soon clambers onto the escarpment, where a slabbed path forking left leads towards the trig point **A**.

Before the last war, the cliffs lay within the Duke of Rutland's grouse shoot and both climbers and ramblers had to keep a wary eye open to avoid the sometimes aggressive discouragements of his gamekeepers. In earlier times, the rock was valued for more practical purposes, its hard, gritty surface rendering it ideal for use as millstones. Great circular 'cheeses' of stone were quarried from the cliffs, but not all were carted away and many still lie among the heather of the lower slopes.

Picking its way among the boulders littering the ridge, the route meanders above the crevices and notches fracturing the cliff below. The superb panorama extends across the Derwent and Hope Valleys, bounded on the western horizon by the plateau of Kinder Scout, the loftiest height of the Peak District National Park. Closer to is

The Cowper Stone

Mam Tor and Lose Hill, with the distinctive peaky top of Win Hill to the right. To the north, the spike of Stanedge Pole breaks the emptiness of the moor, an ancient marker along a highway climbing from Sheffield into Derwent. Records note its existence from the middle of the 16th century, although the tall wooden post is obviously not the original.

After walking ½ mile (800m), watch out for a path branching off left **B**, which drops along an easy rocky gully to a ledge part way down, where you will find a hollow known as Robin Hood's Cave. You can crawl through to a rocky platform, which has a stunning outlook across the landscape.

Climb back to the main path and continue along the ridge, eventually merging with a rough track **C**. It is the old highway previously mentioned, which you can follow to see Stanedge Pole at first hand. Ahead, the track makes a leisurely descent from the ridge, curving to meet a metalled lane at the corner of Dennis Knoll **D**.

The way back to Upper Burbage Bridge lies to the left, keeping left again at successive junctions. Reaching a vergeside parking area beside the second road junction **E**, you have a choice of routes for the final leg. *As an alternative to the last mile left along the road, you can follow an easy path to regain the ridge near the trig point and return along your outward route.* ●

Chelmorton to Deep Dale

		GPS waypoints
Start	Wye Dale, 3 miles (4.8km) east of Buxton on the A6	SK 103 724
Distance	5¼ miles (8.4km)	Ⓐ SK 104 720
Height gain	810 feet (245m)	Ⓑ SK 096 713
Approximate time	2½ hours	Ⓒ SK 096 707
Parking	Car park beside A6 at start (Pay and Display)	Ⓓ SK 100 698
Route terrain	Rocky paths and field tracks	Ⓔ SK 114 702
Ordnance Survey maps	Landranger 119 (Buxton & Matlock), Explorer OL24 (The Peak District – White Peak area)	

For decades, quarry spoil has been dumped at the eastern end of Deepdale, but an ambitious project is underway to restore its native beauty. The work could take until December 2026 to complete, during which time an informal alternative path is provided along the southern rim of the valley. The way requires care, particularly in wet or windy weather, as gradients are steep and there is a sense of exposure above the deep valley.

From the Wye Dale car park, cross the road to a path signed beside the entrance to the Topley Pike Quarry. Passing a line of settling tanks, it quickly enters woodland, where the workings of the quarry are concealed behind high banks. At a fork, bear right through a wicket gate into the Deep Dale Nature Reserve Ⓐ.

A stepped path climbs to a waymarked fork by a bench. The right-hand branch is closed during the restoration works, so continue steeply up the hill to the top wall. Turn right in front of a stile to follow a narrow trod along the rim of the valley. After crossing a fence stile part way along, keep going for almost another ½ mile (800m), before meeting a path emerging through a gate in the accompanying wall. Follow it steeply down to regain the main path along the base of the valley below a small cave Ⓑ. The acclivitous grassy slopes are rich in wild flowers such as bloody cranesbill and bell flower and even the seemingly sterile bands of sharp scree and rocky

Thirst House Cave

outcrops accommodate ferns and the occasional hazel. Higher up, the valley base harbours ash, the dank conditions encouraging swathes of moss upon the boulders. Look out too for Thirst House Cave, where excavations have revealed burials from the Stone Age, the bones of a brown bear and fragments of pottery from the Roman period. Local tales say it is the home of a hob or wood elf and claim that the spring issuing below will cure all ills of those bathing in it upon a Good Friday.

Eventually the restricted bounds of the gorge fall back and the path leaves the nature reserve over a stile. Carry on along a flat meadow at the top of which Horseshoe Dale branches left **C**. Shallower, but still littered with boulders it rises gently towards the plateau, finally passing the even smaller, but private Bullhay Dale, where the cliff is pierced by a double-decker opening, the entrance to an old lead mine. Carry on to the head of Horseshoe

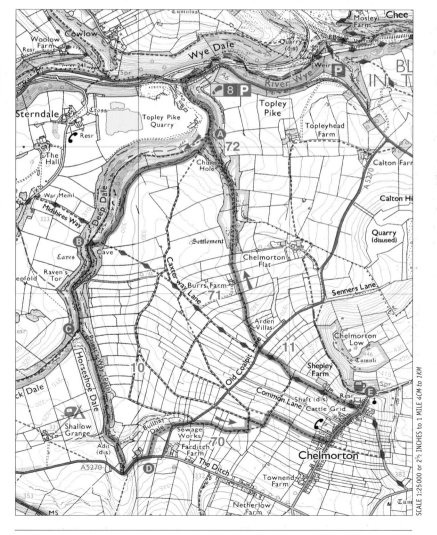

Deep Dale broadens out in its higher reaches

Dale, leaving through a gate by a barn onto the main road.

Go left past Dale Grange Farm, taking to the fields just beyond over a stile on the left **D**. Accompany a broken wall away, bearing right in the next field to return to the road. Follow the verge left for 100 yards before turning right along a green, walled track. Entering a field, turn left to the corner, crossing out onto another track. Go right and then left, looking for a wall stile beside a gate some 70 yards further along on the right. Walk the length of a couple of narrow fields, leaving beside a cottage to emerge on the main street in Chelmorton.

The heart of the village lies to the left, taking you past the Chelmorton Troughs. They are the sole survivors of several stone basins fed by a stream, delightfully named Illy Willy Water, which flowed through the village and provided water until the mains supply finally arrived after the Second World War. Carry on to the top of the lane where the two principal institutions of the community face each other, the **Church Inn** and church, the latter dating from at least the 13th century and having ancient grave markers and coffin lids built into the walls of the Elizabethan porch.

Head a short distance back down the street before turning off right along a track **E** that leads to Shepley Farm. Bear left where it splits and continue between the fields to the main road. Cross to the track's continuation opposite. Through a gate at the end, keep going from field to field, bypassing Burrs Farm. Briefly join a field track, but then, as it curves left, bear off right towards the developing fold of a valley. Beyond a stile the way enters the gorge proper, concealed by trees and dropping steeply to Churn Hole over a rocky step, where those with short legs may need to use their hands. Small caves here yielded a Roman broach and animal bones when excavated at the end of the 19th century. Walk out down the valley to pick up your outward trail at the entrance to the Deep Dale Nature Reserve. ●

The path from Mam Tor to Hollins Cross

Chinley Head

		GPS waypoints
Start	Chinley	SK 040 827
Distance	5½ miles (8.9km)	Ⓐ SK 035 827
Height gain	1,250 feet (380m)	Ⓑ SK 039 830
Approximate time	3 hours	Ⓒ SK 038 834
Parking	Roadside parking in village	Ⓓ SK 036 842
Route terrain	Hill paths and tracks	Ⓔ SK 048 851
Ordnance Survey maps	Landranger 110 (Sheffield & Huddersfield), Explorer OL1 (The Peak District – Dark Peak area)	Ⓕ SK 056 846
		Ⓖ SK 051 834

Chinley lies at the foot of a grassy side-valley on the edge of the Peak District's western hills, its slopes rising either side to give grand views across the surrounding countryside. The walk ascends Chinley Churn, whose upper terrace was once extensively quarried for stone, and continues around the head of the vale of Otterbrook to return along an old track across its eastern flank.

Before the construction of the Peak Forest Canal to Whaley Bridge, Chinley, then known as Maynestonefield was little more than a hamlet. A horse-drawn tramway was built along the Blackbrook Valley connecting the waterway with limestone quarries at Dove Holes, beyond Chapel-en-le-Frith. It also opened a market for the high quality, close-grained gritstone outcropping above Chinley on Cracken Edge, which was sought after for roofing and paving tiles. The dawning industrial age saw the construction of three mills taking their power from the swift-flowing Black Brook, but it was the arrival of the railway in 1867 that really prompted expansion and gave the place its present name, Chinley. Lines to Manchester, London and Sheffield all met here and it became an important junction. The town's proximity to Manchester also made it an attractive proposition to moneyed Victorian commuters, who built their comfortable villas in a country setting away from the grime and overcrowding of the city.

The walk begins from the centre of the village, just east of the station at the junction of Green Lane with the

The quarries of Cracken Edge

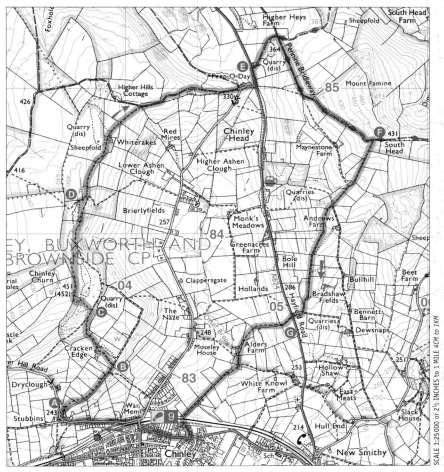

main street, the B6062. Follow Green Lane over a railway bridge to the war memorial and turn left along Stubbins Lane. Beyond houses, the lane gains height past Chinley Nature Reserve and then bends in front of a junction. A short distance after that, look for a waymarked track leaving on the right **A**.

It climbs steeply past a communications mast as a sunken way, but higher up there are glimpses across the Blackbrook Valley to Eccles Pike and on the left to Cracken Edge, the quarried cliffs fringing the summit of Chinley Churn, both tasters of the views to be had during the course of the day. After a good ¼ mile (400m), leave along

a waymarked, gated track on the left **B**.

As the track bends to a farm, walk ahead on a rising grass trod beside a second farm to a small gate. Keep with the left wall to another gate and climb the gorse-covered hillside. Intercepting a broader path higher up, follow it right, soon approaching a fence and stile. However, some 50 yards before it **C**, branch off left on a path that doubles back up the hillside to the foot of the quarries. Now turn right to meet a fence and stile. Immediately over the stile, a faint path off left beside the fence finds

Whiterakes

an easy passage onto the top of the cliffs.

Head north in a delightful saunter along the edge of the cliffs, soaking up the panorama across the Chinley Valley. Beyond the head is Kinder Scout, while behind to the south-west is Shining Tor, which overlooks the upper reaches of the Goyt Valley. Reaching a wall, cross the stile, and at the next wall, continue through the gap. After 100 yards, immediately past a rocky outcrop on the right **D**, fork off right, slanting down to join a broad path below the scarp.

Follow it left, descending easily towards Whiterakes. Keep with the main track beyond the uninhabited farmstead as it arcs right, losing height through a couple of fields to meet another track. To the right, it leads out to the main road beside Peep-O-Day Farm, so named because it catches the first glimmer of the dawn sun rising as it breaks free of the eastern hills.

Follow the verges 150 yards to the left, crossing to a bridleway beside a cottage, Chinley Moor House **E**. After curving past a small quarry, walk up to meet another track. Signed right as the Pennine Bridleway to South Head, it rises easily across the flank of the forlornly named Mount Famine. Stay with it, later bending left past a couple of gates and passing through the gates of a sheep pen a few yards farther on. Keep going beside a wall until, just beyond an intermediate crest, you reach a gate into the National Trust land of South Head **F**.

Do not go through, but instead mount a step stile just before it. Accompany the wall straight down the hill, crossing another stile lower down. Carry on, passing through a gap at the far end of the field. The track then swings left, but you should keep ahead along a narrowing intake to another field. Stick by the left wall above Andrews Farm, going through a gate and shortly joining its access track, which eventually leads out to the main road **G**.

Cross to a stile opposite from which a sunken path continues down the hillside. Through a gate at the bottom, bear left towards Alders Farm. Leave the field through a second gate and walk past the house to join a rough track leading away. After passing beneath the railway, it ultimately emerges onto the B6062 on the edge of Chinley. Go right back to the village centre. ●

Ashford in the Water and Monsal Dale

Ashford in the Water and Monsal Dale

Start	Ashford in the Water	
Distance	6 miles (9.7km)	
Height gain	1,130 feet (345m)	
Approximate time	3 hours	
Parking	Car park in village	
Route terrain	Clear tracks and woodland paths	
Ordnance Survey maps	Landranger 119 (Buxton & Matlock), Explorer OL24 (The Peak District – White Peak area)	

GPS waypoints

- 🖉 SK 194 697
- Ⓐ SK 191 701
- Ⓑ SK 184 715
- Ⓒ SK 181 717
- Ⓓ SK 170 706
- Ⓔ SK 189 694

This superb woodland and riverside walk through Monsal Dale links an idyllic village to one of the finest viewpoints in the Peak District. Of interest is an imposing viaduct condemned by Ruskin and the ruins of an old mill as well as several features in the village itself.

Ashford in the Water is an attractive village of 18th- and 19th-century cottages, built of rugged limestone clustered around a church. The 'water' of its name is the River Wye, and the village grew up at a safe crossing point – a ford by ash trees. In the 17th century the three-arched packhorse bridge, known as the Sheepwash Bridge, was constructed. It is so called because sheep were washed in the river here at shearing time. Although of Norman

Ashford in the Water

Pennyunk Lane

foundation, the church was largely rebuilt in the late 19th century. Inside there is a table of black Ashford 'marble', made from the local common grey limestone, which when polished becomes black and shiny, resembling expensive marble.

📷 Out of the car park behind the church, walk forward along Court Lane to a junction and turn right into Vicarage Lane. After 50 yards double back left on a signed footpath, turning up to climb beside houses and enter a field at the top. Guided by a fingerpost, strike across to find a stile in the far right corner, emerging onto a walled track, Pennyunk Lane Ⓐ.

Follow it left for ³/₄ mile (1.2km), enjoying a splendid vista across the neatly walled rolling countryside. Through a gate at its end, walk away along a contained path. Immediately through a gate at the next corner turn right past a dewpond. Joining the end

of another track keep going forward, soon emerging at a viewpoint above Monsal Dale. Swing right along the lip of the valley, keeping with the path ahead across the steep slope to meet a lane at Monsal Head Ⓑ.

This vantage point, overlooking a right-angled turn of the river, is probably the finest along the valley. The Wye, far below at the bottom of steep-sided, wooded slopes, winds serenely, the whole crossed by a railway viaduct standing prominently in the scene. Victorian conservationists, led by Ruskin, decried it as an ugly intrusive structure, bitterly opposing its construction in 1863 as a desecration of the dale. However, time has weathered the viaduct to harmonise with its surroundings and it has now become one with the landscape. The viaduct carried the Midland Railway route from St Pancras to Manchester, which here ran between Bakewell and Buxton. The railway closed in 1968, but the bridge continues in service as part of the Monsal Trail, a footpath following the course of the Wye from outside Buxton all the way to Bakewell.

Instead of joining the lane, take the descending path signed as access to the viaduct, but at a junction part-way down, keep ahead into Monsal Dale. Reaching the bottom of the valley, turn left through a gate beside a cottage and barn to a footbridge across the river Ⓒ.

Follow the Wye downstream, passing beneath the viaduct to enjoy a delightful walk of some 1¹/₄ miles (2km). As the valley narrows, the path meanders on through a jumble of native woodland. Beyond a weir, the river too takes on a more natural character, swirling in deep pools. Reaching a fork at the edge of the wood, bear left towards White Lodge and the A6.

Emerging onto the main road 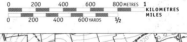, make for the car park opposite. The onward path leaves beside the payment machine, rising through the picnic area to a gate. Keep going over another meadow towards the mouth of Deep Dale, ignoring an intermediate path to Taddington. Joining a stream, briefly follow it up and then cross to a wall stile. Walk directly from the stile on a rising path winding through craggy, open woodland to a junction. Turn left to Ashford and Sheldon, still climbing to another junction in front of a gate.

The route to Ashford lies ahead, now undulating more easily through Great Shacklow Wood. Ignore a crossing path and descend at the edge of the wood to join the river, the way shortly passing the ruin of an old watermill, employed for crushing bones to make fertiliser.

Disregarding the track out to the A6, continue ahead over a stile beside a gate across a succession of meadows, eventually meeting a lane E. Go left to the main road and follow that right for some 300 yards to Sheepwash Bridge. Cross the river back into Ashford and walk ahead along Fennel Street, where you will find the car park on the right, a short way along.

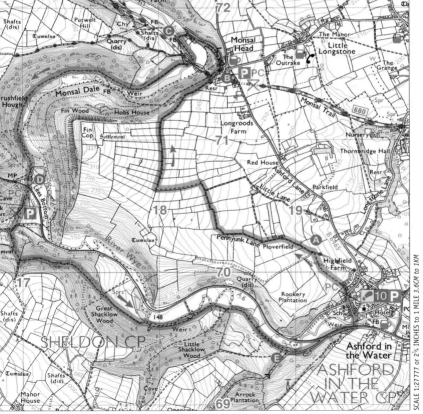

SCALE 1:27777 or 2¼ INCHES to 1 MILE 3.6CM to 1KM

Lyme Park

		GPS waypoints
Start	Lyme Park	🖊 SJ 963 823
Distance	6 miles (9.7km)	Ⓐ SJ 966 830
Height gain	1,000 feet (305m)	Ⓑ SJ 972 821
Approximate time	3 hours	Ⓒ SJ 973 812
Parking	Car park at start	Ⓓ SJ 971 807
Route terrain	Open parkland, moorland paths	Ⓔ SJ 954 805
	and tracks	Ⓕ SJ 948 814
Ordnance Survey maps	Landranger 110 (Sheffield &	Ⓖ SJ 949 816
	Huddersfield), Explorer OL1 (The Peak District – Dark	
	Peak area)	

Lyme Park lies at the edge of the Peak District overlooking the northern Cheshire plain and, although now almost touched by the fringes of the Greater Manchester conurbation, it encompasses a surprisingly vast area of rough grassy hills. This energetic walk traces the high moorland boundary of the estate and is rewarded by extensive panoramas across markedly contrasting landscapes.

For nearly 600 years Lyme Hall belonged to the Legh family, but in 1946 Richard Legh, gave the hall and park to the National Trust. The present mansion replaces an earlier medieval hall and was built during the Tudor period, but then remodelled in the Palladian style in the 1720s by the Italian architect Giacomo Leoni. Its character reflects 18th-century taste and is a treasure trove of fine paintings, furnishings and tapestries.

🖊 Leave the car park by the information centre, taking a graded path

Cluse Hay

that rises to the garden and house. Reaching the courtyard gates, turn left and keep ahead across a junction. Abandon the drive almost immediately, on the bend, and climb a trod ahead. It rises between a sparse avenue of trees along the broad back of a long, grassy hill to a square tower at its far end known as the Cage **A**.

The park was enclosed from the surrounding Macclesfield Forest in 1346 as a private deer park and soon became noted for its fine herd of red deer. Hunting was a popular sport for the Leghs and the Cage was built in the 16th century as a lookout for the ladies to watch the proceedings in comfort. Deer still roam freely across the 1,300 acres (525 ha) of the estate, although they are not always easy to see.

At the foot of the Cage, double back sharp right on a lower swathe, falling along the flank of the hill below the outward path. Before long, at a junction, fork off left across the heath to meet the drive, which you should then follow left past Kennel Wood. Approaching a circular clump of trees, bear off to a fence stile on the right and

The Cage

climb the hill to find a ladder-stile mounting the high wall surrounding Lantern Wood. Walk through the trees, passing above the Lantern, a folly built of stones taken from the Elizabethan hall. Leave the wood at its far end over another ladder-stile, back onto the bare hillside **B**.

Follow the wall up the hill to the top of the wood, turning within the shallow corner to continue along the eastern boundary of the estate. The view extends across the Cheshire plain, where landmarks such as the Jodrell Bank telescope and Alderley Edge can be seen, with the distant hills behind them belonging to Wales. Farther around to the right is the Wirral peninsula and Merseyside, while the conurbation of Greater Manchester nestles at the foot of the Pennine hills.

Marking the high point of the estate, a topograph identifies some of the surrounding features, its plinth extending the panorama by allowing you to see to the east over the tall wall. Keep going until you reach a ladder-stile by a gate, passing out of the park beside a lonely farmhouse to emerge onto the end of a lane **C**.

Just to the left beside the lane are the Bow Stones, believed to be part of the shafts of late Saxon crosses and might have been set here to serve as landmarks or boundary stones. The onward route, however, lies to the right, following a gated, walled track along the hilltop for some 700 yards before breaking out onto the open moor **D**.

Leave the track there, sticking by the right-hand wall; the way signed to Pott Shrigley. Losing height, a track eventually develops which later parts company with the wall and leads to a gate. Just beyond, bear off right, climbing the grassy spoil heaps of old workings to a waymarked fence stile at Dale Top. Over that, walk straight ahead down the hill, guided by a stone wall on your right. Keep going to the bottom to gain a track, Moorside Lane at Keepers Cottage **E**.

Walk right past the cottage and then look for a wall stile by a gate on the left. Signed to Higher Poynton, a trod strikes a shallow diagonal over open grass, later dipping across a tree-lined gully. The continuing path curves to join a wall above a deepening clough, eventually dropping beside an old quarry before emerging onto the end of a track by some houses. Follow it out to a lane beside Green Close Methodist Church **F**.

Go right and then immediately leave the lane along another track, crossing a bridge to West Parkgate Lodge **G**. Turn in front of it through a gate back into the National Trust estate and follow a delightful track winding up a wooded valley, which higher up, in early summer, is ablaze with the colourful flowers of rhododendron. Beyond another gate at the top, carry on with the drive through open parkland to return to the car park below the house. ●

Redmires Reservoirs

		GPS waypoints
Start	Wyming Brook	🖉 SK 268 858
Distance	6 miles (9.7km)	Ⓐ SK 271 855
Height gain	850 feet (260m)	Ⓑ SK 274 853
Approximate time	3 hours	Ⓒ SK 276 845
Parking	Car park at start	Ⓓ SK 256 851
Route terrain	Generally clear paths across open moorland and woodlands	Ⓔ SK 256 856
		Ⓕ SK 257 873
		Ⓖ SK 264 870
Ordnance Survey maps	Landranger 110 (Sheffield & Huddersfield), Explorer OL1 (The Peak District – Dark Peak area)	

Hallam Moors lie barely a mile (1.6km) from the suburbs of Sheffield, yet the heather slopes and forested valleys are a world apart from the populous city. The walk begins along the deserted flanks of Rud Hill above the Redmires Reservoirs and then loops back through the mixed woodlands above the neighbouring Rivelin Valley.

The outbreak of the First World War in 1914 saw many local battalions formed across the country, patriotic fervour and a belief that the war would be over in months bringing no shortage of willing volunteers. Recruiting began on 10 September for the 12th (Service) Battalion of the York and Lancaster Regiment, better known as the Sheffield Pals. Within two days, more than 1,000 local men from all walks of life had joined up. Initial instruction began in the town, but the approach of winter saw the regiment encamped in wooden huts above Redmires with Lancashire lads from Burnley and Accrington.

Conditions were harsh as the men were trained in drill, trench digging and the rudiments of combat, but this helped form a strong bond between them. In May, the Pals were moved to scarcely better conditions on Cannock Chase for further military instruction and, after several more postings, were shipped off

Redmires Lower Reservoir

Reddicar Clough

to Egypt at the end of the year to defend the Suez Canal against a Turkish threat.

The attack never materialised and in the spring of 1916, the battalion was posted to the front line in France. Troops were being massed for a mammoth push against the German lines of the Somme, the Sheffield lads being given the task of taking the small but strategic village of Serre. The massive attack began early on 1 July but within minutes the futility of it all must have been obvious as thousands of men were mown down by machine gun fire. By the end of the first horrific day, almost 600 of the Sheffield Pals had been killed or wounded. The carnage dragged on until November, during which time more than $1\frac{1}{2}$ million men, British, Empire, French and German lost their lives. Although subsequently reinforced, the Pals never recovered and were finally disbanded early in 1918. A memorial stands in the French village of Serre to the Sheffield men who never came home.

Leaving the car park, cross Wyming Brook and head up the hill. At the top, turn into Soughley Lane walking as far as a sharp left bend to find a stile on the right Ⓐ. Follow a track towards the foot of Lower Redmires going left at the end of the wall, over a stile and uphill once more.

As the track levels, keep on until halted by a gate Ⓑ. Mount the stile on the right and walk away at the field edge. Meeting a farm track from Fulwood Booth, turn left past the mounds of an old quarry and follow it out to a lane. Go right, later rounding a bend to leave over a ladder-stile on the right Ⓒ.

Contrary to the line shown on some Ordnance Survey maps, the permitted path takes the right-most of two gates at the far end of the grass track to climb past a storage cistern in the adjacent field. A ladder-stile in the corner advances the path onto the moor, striking to a second stile in a fence ahead. Although initially faint, the way soon gathers tangibility to undulate westward past occasional marker posts across the heather and peat of Rud Hill. Almost straight ahead on the skyline rises the slender staff of Stanedge Pole, while below are the three Redmires Reservoirs, backed by forest plantation.

The peat later gives way to bouldery heath and, above the upper reservoir, the path curves in gentle descent towards its head, shortly passing a boundary stone. Cut with the initials SWW, it was erected by Sheffield Water Works when they constructed the reservoirs in the middle of the 19th century. The path drops to a stile beside a footbridge spanning Fairthorn Clough, across which it leads out to a byway Ⓓ.

Follow it above the head of the upper reservoir to a small car park, immediately beyond which a path is signed off through a hand-gate Ⓔ. It rises beside plantation to rough grazing above, following a wall past an old quarry, which provided stone for the reservoir, and then fording a stream. Over a second rise, continue beyond the wall corner, shortly accompanying another wall to a bridged ditch. Cross the stile next to the gate in front and carry on along a clear path. After the wall curves away, walk on past an isolated clump of rhododendron to reach a waymarked crossing of paths **F**.

Go right along the crest of Head Stone Bank from which there is a glimpse of the Rivelin Reservoir through a gap in the trees. At a fork bear right, dropping towards woodland in Reddicar Clough. The path winds into the thick of the trees, eventually meeting a broad path, Wyming Brook Drive. Follow it right to a bridge spanning Reddicar Brook, immediately after which, a rough path leaves on the right **G**.

Climbing stiffly, it soon crosses the accompanying stream and then swings sharply left on an easier line to the top of the trees. Breaking cover, the way undulates along the steep bank above the forest margin, later dipping into the fringe of trees before finally curving away across the moor to meet the corner of a wall. Pass around the corner and walk on with the wall on your right, eventually losing height to return to the car park. ●

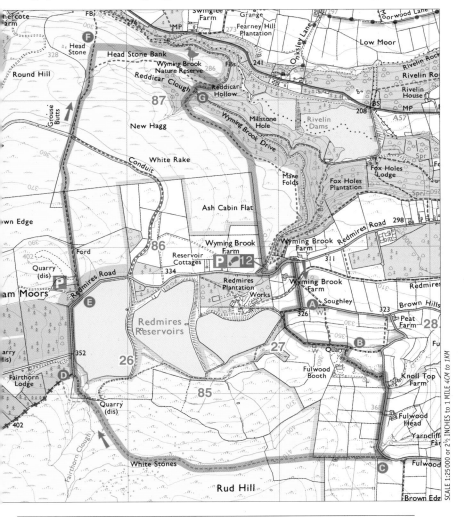

Tissington and Alsop en le Dale

Start	Tissington
Distance	6¼ miles (10.1km)
Height gain	820 feet (250m)
Approximate time	3 hours
Parking	Pay and Display at eastern end of village by Tissington Trail
Route terrain	Field paths and tracks
Ordnance Survey maps	Landranger 119 (Buxton & Matlock), Explorer OL24 (The Peak District – White Peak area)

GPS waypoints

- SK 178 520
- Ⓐ SK 172 526
- Ⓑ SK 164 537
- Ⓒ SK 155 549
- Ⓓ SK 161 551
- Ⓔ SK 182 545
- Ⓕ SK 175 535

This corner of the Peak District abounds in idyllic, unspoiled and uncommercialised villages of warm, honey-coloured limestone, two of the finest being visited in this pleasant ramble. Also featured are two short stretches of the Tissington Trail, a former railway line now usefully converted to a bridleway and giving glorious sweeping views over the surrounding countryside.

Blessed with an avenue of limes where cottages are set back behind wide verges, a church, manorial hall and a pretty pond, Tissington has an air of timeless serenity and seems the quintessential English village. Part of the effect is undoubtedly due to the fact that Tissington is very much an estate village and has been continuously in the possession of one family, the Fitzherberts, since the 15th century. The family still lives in the fine early 17th-century hall, which has been extended and rebuilt several times over the centuries. The simple church, over-looking both hall and village from its mound, retains much Norman work despite a thorough restoration in Victorian times. It possesses a number of monuments to the Fitzherberts, as well as a rare Saxon font. Many of Tissington's cottages date from a rebuilding programme carried out between 1830 and 1860 that included the village school, now a tearoom, built in the year of Queen Victoria's accession (1837).

Although many villages in Derbyshire now hold annual well-dressing ceremonies, none is more associated with this ancient tradition than Tissington. The several wells are decorated with tableaux, which usually depict biblical themes and are made from pressing flowers, ferns, mosses, leaves and bark onto wooden frames covered with clay. The results are strikingly beautiful and ornate. The origins of this custom are somewhat obscure, but the conventional theory is that it started in the middle of the 14th century during the Black Death as a thanksgiving by the villagers for escaping the plague through the purity of the waters. It has not been a continuous custom and may have been first revived in Tissington as a result of the wells not running dry during a great drought in 1615. Whatever the ceremony's origin, well dressing is a colourful spectacle that attracts many visitors to Tissington on Ascension Day and on various dates throughout the summer months to the other villages in the area, which have taken up the custom.

From the car park on the site of the former station, walk up to the lane and keep left to a small green at the village centre. Go right below the church to climb past Tissington Hall. Keep ahead along Rakes Lane until it bends sharply left beyond the village **A**. Quit it there, not along the track in front, but over a stile beside a gate to its left. Strike across the slope, continuing

from field to field and shortly passing above Broadclose Farm. Keep going, negotiating more stiles towards the next farm, Newton Grange. After dropping through a dip, skirt the farm buildings to the right and then curve left to escape from the top corner of the field onto a track. Turn right and subsequently keep ahead to a bridge. Leave just before it through a gate on the right, climbing up to join the Tissington Trail .

This was part of the railway line from Ashbourne to Buxton, which opened in 1899 but finally closed in 1967. Fortunately, the Peak Planning Board swiftly purchased large sections of it (and also other lines that closed around the same time) and created a superb bridleway that runs for 13 miles (21km) between Parsley Hay and Ashbourne, readily accessible by all.

Follow the trail left for about 1 mile (1.6km) to reach a car park. Just past it , look for a stile on the right. Following a sign to Alsop en le Dale, head downhill, crossing the accompanying wall through a gap about halfway along to continue on its opposite flank. Emerging at the bottom over a stile onto a lane, turn right into the village. Although smaller and less frequented than Tissington, it has a similar picturesque combination of attractive Norman church and old hall surrounded by houses, cottages and farms.

Walk through the village to find a stile just past the last house on the left . Climb diagonally across a couple of fields to a stile in the top wall, turning right above it to another stile entering a small coppice wood. At the far side, keep going by a wall and then over further stiles, soon descending through more trees and along the succeeding fields. Eventually meeting a track, cross and make for the bottom right-hand corner of the next field. Through the hedge, go over a second track to find a small gate beneath a holly tree diagonally opposite. Continue at the bottom edge of this final field before leaving through a gate onto a lane. Follow it to the left for a little less than $^1/_4$ mile (400m).

Just past a complex of barns, look for a waymarked stile on the right . Entering a field, head for a narrow gate in the right corner, from which an old, hedged track rises. Through another gate at the top swing right to negotiate a stile, there following the field edge to the left. In the next field, keep going over the hill and then, after crossing the sparse hedge of an old boundary, bear right across the falling slope. Over a bridged ditch resume a direct descent to a bridge spanning the stream that courses the valley bottom. Climb straight up the opposite hill, eventually reaching a gate in the top wall. With the worst of the ascent now behind you, bear half-right to a stile beside a gate .

In front is a railway bridge, but instead of crossing, go over another stile on the left, from which a path slopes to the Tissington Trail. To the left, it leads back to the car park from which the walk began, offering some fine views along the way. ●

One of Tissington's several wells

Digley Reservoir

		GPS waypoints
Start	Digley Reservoir	✐ SE 109 067
Distance	6¼ miles (10.1km)	Ⓐ SE 110 071
Height gain	1,075 feet (330m)	Ⓑ SE 093 073
Approximate time	3 hours	Ⓒ SE 086 072
Parking	Car park at start	Ⓓ SE 087 060
Route terrain	Mainly upland tracks, occasionally rough, *take care in mist*	Ⓔ SE 107 060
Ordnance Survey maps	Landranger 110 (Sheffield & Huddersfield), Explorer OL1 (The Peak District – Dark Peak area)	

Beginning from the Digley Reservoir car park, this fine walk encircles its main tributaries of Marsden Clough and Hey Clough below the steeply rising slopes of Black Hill. It makes use of old trackways, which connected the many isolated farms that once dotted the hillside and whose ruins now stand as reminders of a way of life long gone.

✐ Out of the car park, follow the lane over the dam. At a junction beyond go left, but as the road then bends, leave through a kissing-gate Ⓐ and walk through an old quarry overlooking the foot of the lake. Steps at the far end climb to a walled track, which to the left runs by another quarry and on above the reservoir.

The track existed before the valley was flooded and, after a while, its course dips into the water. The path, however, branches right, shortly dropping steeply down a flight of steps to cross a stream. Rising beyond, the way soon rejoins the old track, which now winds up the hill to a fork above the head of Digley Reservoir. The small lake above Digley is the Bilberry Reservoir, the dam of which failed after unusually heavy rains in 1852, just 12 years after it was completed and flooded the narrow valley below claiming 81 lives.

Take the right branch, eventually climbing to a junction and there go left, contouring the valley side above Marsden Clough. In less than ½ mile (800m), and not far after a gate, look for a path waymarked off on the right Ⓑ. Over a fence stile it rises as an abandoned green way, Old Lane, which is slowly succumbing to the reed tussock that blights the moor, but the extra height repays the effort of passage by opening splendid views back down the Holme Valley and across to the moorland expanses of Holme Moss and Black Hill. It soon curves left to join a track dropping from the main road.

Follow the track up the valley, staying with it as it later swings back around a sharp bend in front of a gate and stile. Continue for a further 50 yards to find a wall stile beside a gate on the right Ⓒ. Accompany the wall downfield, passing through a gate at the bottom from which a grass track drops

The Digley Reservoir

to a bridge spanning the stream at the head of Marsden Clough. Climbing beyond, the track soon veers away to cross the spur of moorland called Good Bent.

Ahead, peeping over the skyline is the Holme Moss transmitter mast, which at 750 feet (229m) high is a landmark from much of the northern Peakland high ground. It is the second mast to occupy the site, the original being put up in 1951 to broadcast BBC television. ITV did not appear until 1956 and for Yorkshire, was transmitted from Emley Moor 8 miles away to the north-east. By 1985, a second mast had been erected alongside to broadcast VHF radio and, more lately, digital radio as well. It is one of the most powerful VHF transmitters in the country and its exceptional height (the base of the mast is already 1,720 feet (524m) above sea level) enables an unrivalled area of coverage.

Broaching the crest, the path bends above Hey Clough and makes for the brooding bulk of Black Hill. Eventually passing a solitary stone gate post **D**, the path dips across the stream and continues briefly above the opposite

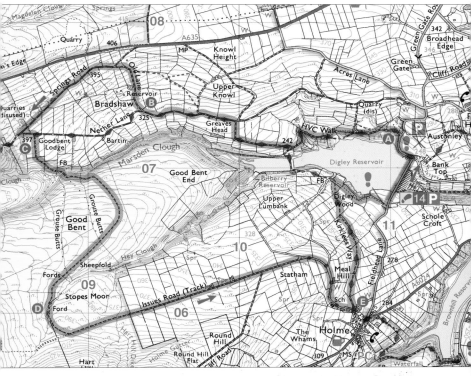

bank before curving back towards the geometric enclosures, seen earlier from the top of Good Bent.

Through a gate, the way continues easily as a broad drove between the walled fields, running dead straight for nearly ¾ mile (1.2km). Tracks join first from the right and then the left before the drove curves in steepening descent past a row of stone cottages and then the village school. Remaining with the lane will take you into Holme, where you will find the village pub, the **Fleece Inn**, just along to the right. The way back, however, lies along a waymarked track, which leaves through a gate on the left beside a barn, 100 yards beyond the school **E**.

Entering a field at the end, bear right to a stile in the far, lower corner and carry on beside the wall at the bottom of the next field as the Digley Reservoir comes into view. A guiding trod leads on over a succession of stiles, eventually intercepting a gravel path above the lake's southern shore. To the right it leads back to the car park.

Nether Lane

Black Moss and Butterley Reservoir

		GPS waypoints
Start	Marsden	
Distance	6¼ miles (10.1km)	🖉 SE 047 118
Height gain	1,080 feet (330m)	Ⓐ SE 043 109
Approximate time	3 hours	Ⓑ SE 026 094
Parking	Standedge Visitor Centre car park by Marsden station	Ⓒ SE 052 088 Ⓓ SE 048 107
Route terrain	Good moorland paths, *take care in mist*	
Ordnance Survey maps	Landranger 110 (Sheffield & Huddersfield), Explorer OL1 (The Peak District – Dark Peak area)	

Two main tributary valleys come together at Marsden to feed the River Colne, that flows from the south having its highest source at 1,670 feet (509m) on Wessenden Moor. Although not venturing quite that far, the route climbs to the Black Moss watershed for a glimpse into old Lancashire before dropping back to the town past a string of reservoirs in the Wessenden Valley.

The highest settlement in the Colne Valley, Marsden grew beside a network of packhorse routes and a coach road crossing the Pennines between Huddersfield and Manchester, which was built in 1760 by Blind Jack Metcalfe of Knaresborough. Within 80 years, canal and railway followed, transforming the place from a tiny hamlet into a booming industrial town. The cottagers abandoned their hand-looms to work in the mills and iron works, of which at one time there were 30 crowded into the constricted valley. The prosperity provided money for the large church dedicated to St Bartholomew, built in 1895 to replace an earlier chapel that had stood across the road. There were other public buildings too, including a Mechanics Institute, where the working men sought to better themselves by education. Restored and still used for adult education and community events, its distinctive clock tower rises as a landmark above the town's roofs.

🖉 Leaving the car park facing **The Railway** pub, walk down Station Road and bear right over a bridge and past St Bartholomew's Church. Keep right along Towngate, cross the main road and continue up Old Mount Road opposite, which climbs steeply out of the town. Leaving the cottages behind, the view opens across the foot of the Wessenden Valley, where the high dam of the Butterley Reservoir is a prominent feature. After almost ½ mile (800m), the gradient eases by a cluster of cottages. Look for a narrow footpath Ⓐ signed off between them (not the track doubling back just before), which rises to the open hillside behind. Carry on beside a wall, passing through a gate at the top onto a higher track. Follow it left, rejoining the lane and walking a few yards further to a second junction.

Cross to a narrow path opposite, which drops awkwardly to cross a brook. Gaining height out of the gully, the path broadens and strikes south-west across the moor. Over to the right is Pule Hill, its flanks pocked and scarred by stone quarries, while ahead the Redbrook Reservoir shortly comes into sight. After $^3/_4$ mile (1.2km) of easy walking the path dips to ford a stream.

Ascend to the track above where you will find a prominent marker stone just to the left **B**.

There, go right and re-cross the stream, climbing away across the moor on a good, slabbed path. Passing through a kissing-gate, the tussock yields to heather, which rises to a second fence just beyond the skyline. Although hardly a prominent hill, the

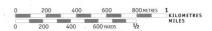

Marsden from Clark Hill

panorama is extensive. Behind is the long ridge of Standedge overlooking the mill towns of eastern Lancashire, while ahead, some 5 miles (8km) distant is the Holme Moss transmitter, broadcasting radio to much of Yorkshire. Leaving the top the way falls to a diminutive body of water, the Black Moss Reservoir.

Approaching the low dam, swing left beside the reservoir, which curiously straddles the watershed and has a retaining wall at either end. Drawing level with its eastern wall, turn right across the bund and a footbridge. Curving left, the continuing path wanders past the neighbouring Swellands Reservoir over the undulating moor. The way gradually falls beside the deepening rift of Blakely Clough, bringing the high dam of the Wessenden Reservoir into view. After descending more steeply, the path fords the stream just below a weir. A broader track carries on along the opposite flank, ending by a small, covered cistern from which there is a superb vista along the Wessenden Valley **C**.

A narrow path drops steeply to a bridge spanning Wessenden Brook. *You can then either climb to the service track and follow that down the valley or,*
alternatively, continue beside the brook and along the shore of Blakeley Reservoir, joining the track later beside the dam. Carry on past the Butterley Reservoir to meet a lane.

A few yards to the left **D**, look for a path descending a long flight of steps to a turning area by garages and a house. Bear right to leave along a track, which soon runs between the tall buildings of one of the many mills that brought Victorian prosperity to the town. Emerging past a terrace of cottages walk left and continue ahead over a roundabout junction along Fall Lane. Approaching the main road, branch off left to pass beneath a bridge. Keep left again into Towngate and retrace your outward steps past the church to the car park.

Marsden's wealth was founded on wool, the fast-flowing streams coursing off the moors powering textile mills along the valley. As the industrial age gathered pace, many expanded and were converted to steam, fuelled by coal brought in along the canal and then by the railway. In the town, Enoch and James Taylor turned their blacksmith trade to making cropping frames, which were used to finish the cloth. However, the mechanising revolution was not a bloodless affair, and there was plenty of opposition to the new-fangled factory machinery that took the work out of the cottages. The Luddites attacked many of the new mills in Lancashire and Yorkshire, smashing the machines to the cry 'Enoch makes 'em and Enoch breaks 'em', alluding to the fact that his firm also made the sledgehammers wielded by the destructive gangs. ●

Castleton and Mam Tor

		GPS waypoints
Start	Castleton	
Distance	6¼ miles (10.1km)	🖉 SK 149 829
Height gain	1,325 feet (405m)	Ⓐ SK 150 827
		Ⓑ SK 135 813
Approximate time	3 hours	Ⓒ SK 125 814
Parking	Car park at western edge of town – Pay and Display	Ⓓ SK 126 826
		Ⓔ SK 125 833
		Ⓕ SK 136 845
Route terrain	Generally clear upland paths and tracks	
Ordnance Survey maps	Landranger 110 (Sheffield & Huddersfield), Explorer OL1 (The Peak District – Dark Peak area)	

Castleton occupies an enviable position near the head of the Hope Valley, dominated by the ruins of Peveril Castle and surrounded by bold hills and rolling moors. The walk begins with a long, steady ascent of Cave Dale to the gently undulating stone-walled fields above. There is then a sharp but short pull onto the 1,695 feet (517m) summit of Mam Tor, which begins one of the finest scenic ridge walks in the Peak District. Linger to enjoy the views into the Vale of Edale and the Hope Valley, but save enough time to visit one of the nearby caves or perhaps, despite the daunting-looking climb, explore the castle ruins.

Surrounded by fantastic scenery and a multitude of attractions, it is little wonder that Castleton has become one of the principal tourist centres of the Peak District. The town grew up around the foot of Peveril Castle, which was founded in the late 11th century by William Peverel, an illegitimate son of William the Conqueror. The stronghold occupies a virtually impregnable position, with steep cliffs on three sides. It seems likely that initially a curtain wall was constructed only on the north side overlooking the town and that the other flanks relied on the natural defence afforded by the cliffs. The castle's most outstanding feature is the great keep, built by Henry II in 1176

after it had been forfeited to the Crown. But it was not solely a defensive fortress, as it also served as a hunting lodge for the Royal Forest of the Peak before falling into disuse and subsequent ruin in the 15th century.

The predominant building in the village itself is the church, which, though mainly a 19th-century restoration, retains its fine Norman chancel arch. However, the sites drawing the greatest number of visitors to Castleton are the varied and spectacular caverns that honeycomb the surrounding hills. They are, in fact a mixture of natural caves and man-made tunnels, created as a result of mining for lead and other minerals. There are four show caves to

Heading down to Hollins Cross

emerge onto a broad track **B**.

Go right through a gate and, when you shortly reach a fork, take the track ahead. Carry on for almost another $^1/_2$ mile (800m) to the far side of the second large field. Ignore the gate ahead and instead mount a stile on the right **C**.

choose from: the Peak, Blue John, Treak Cliff and Speedwell Caverns, the latter being particularly exciting as it involves a subterranean boat trip.

After wandering around the exhibitions in the Castleton Centre beside the car park, follow the main street through the town as far as a sharp left-hand bend. Peak Cavern and Peveril Castle are signed off to the right, the road taking you past the church to a green in the middle of the old market place. Take the lane to the left at the top, but almost immediately, look for a bridleway to Cave Dale leaving between cottages on the right **A**.

The path, sandwiched between abrupt rocky portals, winds up the narrow gorge, passing below the ruins of Peveril Castle perched high on the lip above. Beyond a gate at the head of the gorge, the way continues more easily through the upper part of the dale, eventually turning through a gate in the right-hand wall. Carry on to another gate and then at a waymark just beyond, bear left over the crest of the field, where the view right is to Mam Tor, the ramparts and ditches of its Iron Age summit fort evident even from here. Closer to hand, the landscape is pockmarked with the tips of old lead mines, which often broke through to the natural caves below. Pass through a gated sheep pen in the far corner to

Follow the left-hand wall away past grass-covered mounds that betray more abandoned workings. Mam Tor, now seen in front of you, is known as the 'Shivering Mountain' on account of instability in its lower layers of loose, soft shales, which are constantly crumbling and falling, giving the impression that the hill is moving or shivering. A landslide some years ago led to the closure of the A625 Sheffield to Chapel-en-le-Frith road and light traffic is now diverted through Winnats Pass, a steep and narrow route between towering limestone cliffs. Over a couple of stiles the onward way then falls gently downhill, leading to a gate onto a lane near the head of Winnats Pass **D**.

Cross diagonally right to a gate (not the one directly opposite) and follow a field track that shortly meets another road. Through a small gate opposite, a path rises enthusiastically ahead up the grassy hill, culminating in steps onto the Edale road **E**.

Instead of following the road, go through a gate on the right from which a stepped path takes you to the summit of Mam Tor. The views from the top are magnificent: to the north is the Vale of Edale from which the Pennine Way can be seen clearly snaking up onto Kinder Scout, and to the east you can just spot Peveril Castle above Castleton, with the Hope Valley winding between the hills beyond. The onward route lies ahead,

an exhilarating ridge walk along the spine of the hill, overlooking a patchwork of hedged green fields speckled with trees, while scattered across the hillside are lonely farmsteads and cottages. The path gently loses height for ¾ mile (1.2km) before reaching Hollins Cross, a junction of ancient paths marked by a stone cairn **F**.

Although the ridge path continues on to Lose Hill (alternatively known as

Ward's Piece after a Sheffield man, G. H. B. Ward, who made a major contribution to the cause of rambling in the area), we now leave it, branching off right to drop across the steep hillside in the direction of Castleton. Initially paved, it descends over stiles, eventually joining a sunken path that ends at a farm track. Follow it ahead, keeping right where it later forks to pass an outdoor centre. Beyond there a lane leads to the town. Go forward when you meet the main road, bending right with it through the centre to return to the car park. ●

The Manifold Valley

Start	Wetton	GPS waypoints
Distance	6½ miles (10.5km)	◢ SK 109 551
Height gain	1,420 feet (435m)	Ⓐ SK 109 554
Approximate time	3½ hours	Ⓑ SK 104 572
Parking	Car park at edge of village	Ⓒ SK 095 584
Route terrain	Field paths and valley trails, steep descent to Ecton	Ⓓ SK 091 577
		Ⓔ SK 098 550
Ordnance Survey maps	Landranger 119 (Buxton & Matlock), Explorer OL24 (The Peak District – White Peak area)	

The Manifold flows roughly parallel with the Dove through similarly attractive limestone scenery, but its valley is generally quieter and less well known. The name Manifold means literally many folds or turns and is an apt one, for the river forms a whole series of loops and meanders along its length. From the village of Wetton the route takes an undulating course across the fields, passing the remains of abandoned copper mines and eventually climbing to a most dramatic and expansive viewpoint overlooking the Manifold Valley. After a steep descent into the dale there is a lovely walk along the Manifold Track, a disused railway line that keeps by the winding river. The return to Wetton passes the impressive Thor's Cave, without doubt the dominant feature of the surrounding landscape.

The small, remote and seemingly unchanging village of Wetton lies on the eastern slopes of the Manifold Valley, its attractive grey stone cottages grouped around a pub and medieval church, a short and plain building with a rather heavy-looking tower.

◢ From the car park turn left along a lane and left again at a road junction, walking through the village to pass the **Royal Oak Inn** and then the church. Where the road bends left, bear off along a track, which is subsequently signed to Back of Ecton Ⓐ. Through a gateway at the top, walk ahead negotiating a couple of gap stiles to

gain the National Trust land of Wetton Hill. A grassy trod guides you from field to field, soon meeting and following a wall below the flanks of Wetton Hill as a grand view opens ahead.

Remain with the wall until it turns, there keeping ahead towards the far bottom field corner. Walk forward across the marshy gatherings of a stream to a stile, climbing to a gate, just left of the top-right corner of the field beyond. Go right to meet a lane Ⓑ. Turn left, zigzagging up the hill to leave just before the brow through a gate on the right. Head diagonally up, joining a wall that guides you to the abandoned ruins of a copper mine. The ore deposits were some of the richest in Europe and the shafts and levels honeycombing the hill made a fortune for the fifth Duke of Devonshire. Carry on over a stile, initially beside a wall and then breaking from it to make a beeline past the spoil tips of more workings for a triangulation pillar on the summit of Ecton Hill. From it, the ground falls dramatically into the Manifold Valley with the village of Warslow topping the opposite hill. Beneath your feet are Dale Bridge and a curious house, more reminiscent of the Rhineland than Staffordshire.

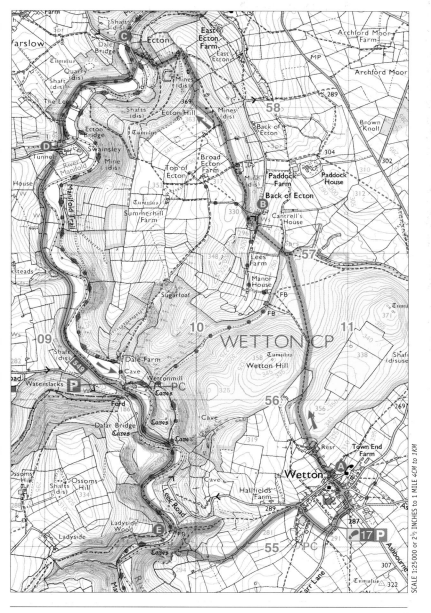

The Manifold Valley

After a little over ½ mile (800m), the way joins a lane **D**. Keep going through a tunnel, following the lane beyond for a further mile (1.6km) to a junction opposite Wetton Mill. The mill, accessed over an old packhorse bridge, ground corn until it closed in 1857 but now restored by the National Trust, continues as a **tearoom** and holiday cottages.

Bear right along the escarpment, passing through a gap in the corner of a broken wall to descend to a narrow gate. Proceed downhill past more mine workings, turning the corner in front of a stone building, built in 1788 to house a steam engine designed by James Watt. The way continues straight down the ever-steepening hill bringing you to a wall at the bottom, which is crossed by a stile at its right-hand end. Turn right to pass beneath an arch abutting the whimsical house seen from the top of the hill and follow a track out to the lane by Dale Bridge. Cross the lane as if to go over the bridge, but turn off left just before it through a gate onto the Manifold Track **C**.

Created in 1937 by Staffordshire County Council, the path follows the disused Leek and Manifold Light Railway. The single-track line carried mainly milk and also a few tourists, but enjoyed only a brief existence between 1904 and 1934. Its course now provides a splendid passage for cyclists and walkers and as you follow the winding river, it is easy to see how the magnificent valley came by its name.

Resume the riverside trail below sheer limestone cliffs, shortly crossing the river. At a junction, keep ahead over another bridge, beyond which Thor's Cave soon comes into view, a gaping hole high in the cliff overlooking the narrow gorge. Approaching its foot, abandon the track **E** for a footbridge across the river.

On the other side, the path climbs away through dense woodland, eventually rising to a junction where a side path is signed to Thor's Cave. It rises steeply to the cavern's yawning entrance, from which there is a magnificent view back along the valley. Archaeological excavations have revealed that it was inhabited during prehistoric times, a haven offering both shelter and security.

Turn as if to retrace your steps, but immediately bear right on a path that contours around the rock to a gate. Keep ahead along the undulating boundary of sloping fields, shortly reaching a wall stile out onto the end of an enclosed track. Follow it left towards Wetton. Meeting a lane, walk right, almost immediately going right again at a junction. Turn left at the end to return to the car park. ●

The Goyt Valley and Shining Tor

		GPS waypoints
Start	Errwood Reservoir	🖉 SK 012 748
Distance	6½ miles (10.5km)	Ⓐ SK 001 761
Height gain	1,310 feet (400m)	Ⓑ SJ 995 767
Approximate time	3½ hours	Ⓒ SJ 994 737
Parking	Car park at start. On bank holidays and summer Sundays park at Pym Chair and begin from Ⓑ because of road closures	Ⓓ SK 000 729
		Ⓔ SK 011 730
		Ⓕ SK 011 735
Route terrain	Generally clear moorland paths	
Ordnance Survey maps	Landrangers 118 (Stoke-on-Trent & Macclesfield) and 119 (Buxton & Matlock), Explorer OL24 (The Peak District – White Peak area)	

The character of the Goyt Valley has altered over the last half-century. The vale's former isolation has ebbed before an influx of car-borne visitors and its natural lines changed by the construction of reservoirs and planting of conifers. Despite these intrusions upon the moorland, woods and streams, it remains a valley of outstanding beauty, the lakes and forests another facet of diversity. This walk encompasses its most interesting features and grandest scenery, climbing past the scanty ruins of an abandoned hall and unusual shrine. An airy ridge walk to the summit of Shining Tor reveals splendid views on both sides before the way drops back into the wooded valley.

The Goyt Valley was formerly a remote area of wild and open country lying between two royal hunting grounds, Peak Forest to the east and Macclesfield Forest to the west. It was partially 'tamed' in the 19th century, both by the activities of the Grimshawe family, who built Errwood Hall and laid out the surrounding ornamental gardens and by the growth of industry in the area, notably quarrying and coal-mining. More major and significant changes to its landscape took place during the last

century with the damming of the river by Stockport Corporation to create two reservoirs, Fernilee in 1938 and Errwood in 1967 and, from 1963, the Forestry Commission's planting of large blocks of conifers, mainly on the western slopes.

🖉 Leave the rear of the car park by an information board, climbing the grassy slope to a gap in the upper wall. Go right on a track that shortly curves left through a steep and narrow wooded valley. Part-way up, turn sharp right, soon passing below the ruins of

Looking back from Oldgate Nick

Errwood Hall. It was built in 1830 by the Grimshawes, a Roman Catholic family who owned much of the valley and contemporary photographs show a handsome and palatial, Italian-looking residence surrounded by exotic landscaped gardens. However, the hall was abandoned and demolished in the 1930s as the waters of the first of the reservoirs started to rise. Today, the meagre ruins retain an attractively melancholic air, but rhododendrons and azaleas, vestiges of the ornamental gardens, still bloom resplendent during late May and June.

The path continues above a stream, shortly dipping to cross. On the far bank, turn right and then left at successive junctions to climb below Foxlow Edge, the way signed towards the Shrine and Pym Chair. There is an excellent view of the ridge soon to be traversed before you reach the Spanish Shrine, a simple, circular building of local gritstone but undeniably Mediterranean in inspiration and design. It was erected by the Grimshawes in 1889 in memory of a much-loved Spanish governess in their employ.

Beyond the shrine the path rises steadily and it is then not far to the lane **Ⓐ**. Turn up the hill but leave as you approach the brow through a gate in the wall on the left **Ⓑ**.

The viewpoint, known as Pym Chair, commands a superb panorama over the Goyt woodlands and surrounding hills. It lies at the crossing of ancient routes, one of which was a 'saltway' from the Cheshire salt-producing district around Northwich and Nantwich that ran across the Pennines to Chesterfield and Sheffield.

Through the gate, a path signed to Shining Tor climbs and settles along the ridge beside a stone wall. It offers a grand walk for over $1^{3}/_{4}$ miles (2.8km), rising first over Cats Tor (1,703 feet/519m) and then onto Shining Tor (1,833 feet/559m), where a triangulation pillar marking the summit lies over a ladder-stile to the right **Ⓒ**. There is a splendid view in all directions across the rolling hills and bare moorlands, the distinctive conical shape of Shutlingsloe clearly visible, some three miles (4.8km) to the south.

Returning to the path, follow it down across a saddle to a kissing-gate, through which is a crossing path. Turn right, shortly passing through a gate to find, immediately beyond, a stile on the left **Ⓓ**. Signed to Goyt's Clough Quarry, a path drops beside a wall. Reaching the corner of a forest, which is being progressively harvested and replanted, the way skirts its perimeter, in time crossing a track into the plantation. Ignore it and keep going outside the fence until eventually, you reach a stile. Cross and follow a winding path down to a bridge spanning a stream. Climb left to a fork above the far bank **Ⓔ** and keep left on a permissive path that tacks above the brook falling through Deep Clough, coming out at the bottom onto a narrow lane by the abandoned quarries.

You can then simply follow the lane left back to the car park, but a more interesting path can be found a short way along as you enter a stand of trees **F**. Signed off right as the Riverside Walk, it drops to follow the Goyt downstream, returning later to the lane.

Cross diagonally to the gated continuation of the track, now signed to Errwood Hall. It rises above the lane and later, the car park, which is then signed off as you approach.

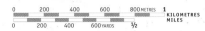

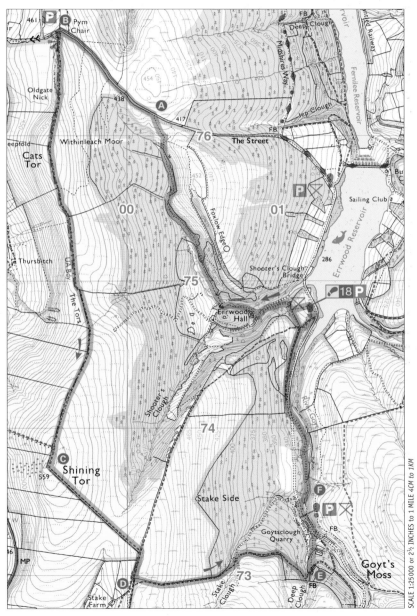

Cromford and Matlock Bath

Cromford and Matlock Bath

		GPS waypoints
Start	Cromford Wharf	
Distance	7 miles (11.3km)	☑ SK 299 570
Height gain	1,390 feet (425m)	Ⓐ SK 300 572
Approximate time	3½ hours	Ⓑ SK 300 586
Parking	Pay and Display at start	Ⓒ SK 297 583
Route terrain	Woodland paths and tracks, narrow lane	Ⓓ SK 293 580
		Ⓔ SK 295 569
Ordnance Survey maps	Landranger 119 (Buxton & Matlock), Explorer OL24 (The Peak District – White Peak area)	Ⓕ SK 298 561
		Ⓖ SK 293 557
		Ⓗ SK 313 559

An incredible variety of scenic and historic attractions are packed into this absorbing walk. The natural wonders include the narrow Derwent gorge and the impressive Black Rock above Cromford. Equally striking is the Victorian architecture of Matlock Bath, the fascinating mill settlement of Cromford and the railway incline dropping to the Cromford Canal, where the former workshops house an interesting museum.

In 1771 Sir Richard Arkwright, a Lancashire cotton entrepreneur, established the first successful water-powered cotton mill in the then scattered farming community of Cromford – an event which helped transform textile manufacturing from a cottage-based craft into a factory-located industry. Arkwright chose Cromford because of the power of the River Derwent, but it did have two disadvantages: a shortage of labour and poor communications. He created a village to bring people from the surrounding countryside, but the second difficulty was never completely overcome. Although he built a canal, which was later linked by railway to the Peak Forest Canal at Whaley Bridge, Cromford was far from the sea ports through which raw cotton and finished goods were traded. Unable to compete

effectively with the main centres of the cotton industry, the town never developed into another Manchester or Bolton. However, what remains is a rare example of an early Industrial Revolution textile settlement, which has retained many of the original buildings erected by Arkwright and his successors. Some of these can be found near the start of the walk, which begins at the head of the canal opposite Arkwright's Mill. The complex dates from the late 18th century and is being restored by the Arkwright Society.

🖋 Turn right past the church, founded towards the end of the 18th century as a private chapel for the Arkwrights and where Sir Richard was buried. It was enlarged in the 19th century to accommodate the growing community. Across the bridge is the entrance to Willersley Castle, once

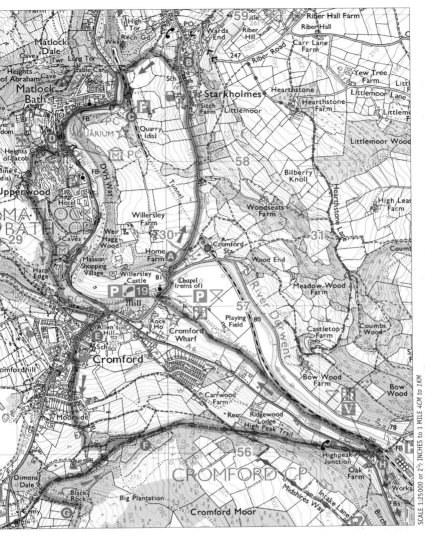

SCALE 1:25000 or 2½ INCHES to 1 MILE 4CM to 1KM

home to the industrialist and now a hotel. Fork left just past there up a steep lane to Starkholmes **A**; be aware of traffic for the lane is narrow and has no footway. Where it later levels, a fine view opens across the valley to Matlock Bath. Reaching the village, look for a footpath on the left, just before the **White Lion B**.

Doubling back, wind down the hillside, joining another path at the edge of a wood. Beyond the Heights of Abraham cable car station, pass beneath a railway bridge and turn left beside the river to a bridge opposite Matlock Bath Station **C**.

The arrival of the railway helped Matlock Bath develop as a popular spar, bringing Victorians to take the waters in the Pavilion and Pump Room and enjoy the riverside gardens and scenery, still appreciated today.

Follow the main road left to the

On top of Black Rock

Pavilion, crossing to a footpath beside the **Fishpond pub** (D). At the top go right past the entrance to the Gulliver's Kingdom Theme Park, leaving just beyond where a path is signed left to Upperwood. Briefly join the theme park's rising drive, but leave in a few yards for another path on the right. After 100 yards, turn left onto a stepped path that climbs the steep hillside to emerge onto a lane.

Go left through the hamlet of Upperwood, bearing left at a fork. Beyond the houses, keep ahead as the way degrades to a track and then a footpath, a signpost directing you towards Scarthin. The ongoing path falls gradually across a wooded hillside, where in spring you will find celandine, wood anemone, wood sorrel and ramsons. Lower down, keep ahead and then bear right at consecutive junctions, passing behind a large hotel. Beside the road far below is Masson Mill, begun by Sir Richard Arkwright in 1783-4.

The path shortly curves across the rib of the hill, zigzagging down the opposite flank to emerge in the former lead-mining settlement of Scarthin. Walk left through the village to the main road (E).

Turn up the hill in the direction of Cromford, passing North Street. Built in 1776 to accommodate Arkwright's

workforce, the three-storey terraces are regarded as Britain's earliest planned industrial housing and were greatly in advance of their time. Continue for another 200 yards to find a narrow alley on the left, Beedhouse Lane, which then curves right behind house gardens. Meeting a street, the ongoing track opposite is signed to Black Rock. At the top of that, walk left on a narrow lane. Bend right and then go left at the next junction, continuing beyond a house on a grass track into a wood. Through a gate, a path winds past a disused quarry before ending at a couple of stiles. Clamber over the one on the right to gain the old trackbed of the former Cromford and High Peak Railway (F).

Black Rock lies $^1/_2$ mile (800m) to the right. Reaching a car park, take a path on the left. It climbs to the top of the impressive outcrop of weatherworn gritstone boulders from which there is a splendid panoramic view across the countryside (G).

Descend and go back along the railway, continuing beyond (F) to pass the old winding house at Sheep Pasture. It was built in 1830 to haul wagons up and down the $^3/_4$ mile (1.2km) 1 in 8 incline to High Peak Junction beside the Cromford Canal. At the end of the track, the restored workshops in the marshalling yard house an interesting museum. Cross a canal bridge to join the towpath (H).

If you have the time, a short walk to the right takes you to the Leawood Pump House, built in 1849 to lift water from the River Derwent into the Cromford Canal. The return, however, is to the left, a pleasant one-mile (1.6km) stroll beside the waterway back to Cromford Wharf. ●

A Five Dales Walk

Start	Tideswell
Distance	6¾ miles (10.9km)
Height gain	1,250 feet (380m)
Approximate time	3½ hours
Parking	Roadside parking in village
Route terrain	Field and woodland paths, the flood diversion ends in a brief but awkward clamber
Ordnance Survey maps	Landranger 119 (Buxton & Matlock), Explorer OL24 (The Peak District – White Peak area)

GPS waypoints

- 🖊 SK 152 757
- Ⓐ SK 165 751
- Ⓑ SK 175 744
- Ⓒ SK 173 727
- Ⓓ SK 157 731
- Ⓔ SK 154 745

The five dales featured here are: Tansley, Cressbrook, Water-cum-Jolly, Miller's and Tideswell, each attractive and having a distinctive character. The walk begins at a fine church known as the 'Cathedral of the Peak' built on the wealth derived from wool and lead. There is evidence too of former industrial activity along the banks of the Wye in the imposing water-powered mills at Cressbrook and Litton, although today it is once again Nature that holds sway in the dales.

Tideswell is one of those places that is difficult to categorise – for although barely larger than a village, it has all the bustle and appearance of a lively town. Tideswell developed during the later part of the Middle Ages as an important market and lead-mining centre and its imposing church, justifiably dubbed the 'Cathedral of the Peak', was built during its heyday. Dedicated to St John the Baptist, it is predominantly a 14th-century building with a fine porch and tall, pinnacled west tower. Unusually for a village church, it has two transepts. Inside, it is spacious and dignified with old tombs and ornate 19th-century wood carving that would put many a parish church in much larger towns to shame. With the decline of the mining industry, the place faded into relative obscurity, leaving the church to remind us of its prosperous past.

🖊 Begin from the church, crossing the road to turn right. At a fork in front of the bank, branch left along Church Street, following that for 50 yards before turning left up a narrow passage at the end of the first terrace of houses. Climb steps at the back to a track above the houses and follow it left out to a lane. To the right, it leads over the hill to Litton, ¾ mile (1.2km) away. Meeting the main road, go left through the village, its 17th- and 18th-century stone cottages set back behind broad grass verges. Towards the far end, turn off right at Litton View, passing beside the farmhouse to a stile on the left immediately behind, Ⓐ.

Signed to Cressbrook Dale and Wardlow, a trod strikes out across the field to a walled track at the far side. A

Cressbrook Mill has been restored as residential apartments

few yards to the left, is a stile on the right. Walk down the narrow field, curving around the bottom-left wall corner and dropping to another stile. Beyond, a path falls past the pockmarks of old mine workings, following the deepening gorge of Tansley Dale to its junction with Cressbrook Dale. Over a stile at the bottom, a plank bridge provides an occasionally necessary crossing of the streambed, then turn right. Almost immediately, the path forks, the higher branch rising determinedly past a shuttered mine shaft to the top of the eastern flank of the valley **B**. *You can alternatively stay with the path along the valley floor, although the climb is amply rewarded by a splendid view along the dale with the cottages and farms of Litton still visible on the horizon.*

Approaching the top, fork right to a gate and follow the sloping path back into the dale, dropping through coppiced woodland to rejoin the bottom track. A little farther on, the path crosses a footbridge then twists left into bushes. Immediately, turn off right to climb steeply beside a wall at the edge of trees. As the gradient eases, keep ahead across the grass, from where there is a view to the almost perpendicular cliffs enclosing the other

side of the dale. A track develops, which leads on through a wood, shortly emerging onto a lane. Follow it downhill to Cressbrook, there turning in at the service entrance to the converted mill to pick up a fenced path to Litton Mill **C**.

Skirt the rear of Cressbrook Mill, which was built in 1815, but more recently became almost derelict before it was developed as a housing complex. The path turns away beside the old leat that once fed the waterwheels to a junction below the expansive millpond. Bear right, crossing the leat to follow a path around the back of the pond beneath a high overhanging limestone cliff, a favourite practice ground for rock climbers. Continue upstream beside the River Wye through the delightful and oddly named Water-cum-Jolly Dale.

*A flooding river may occasionally render the path beneath the cliff impassable. In which case, return to the road, Point **C**, go left and immediately fork left to climb steeply away. After some 200 yards, just beyond the last house, slip through a gap in the left wall. Contour the wooded bank above the cliffs to pass below Cressbrook Hall. The path then descends the steepening slope back into trees, finishing in a short clamber to rejoin the main path.*

As the river narrows, the valley becomes Miller's Dale, the path passing the remains of one of its old mills. It is a lovely place, where the steep grassy meadows above fall to sheer cliffs that enclose the swift flowing river and a bordering strip of wetland wood. Eventually reaching Litton Mill, which, like Cressbrook, has been renovated for accommodation, the way winds across the tailrace to climb between the factory and mill-workers' cottages. Carry on for a further $\frac{1}{4}$ mile (400m) along a lane, quitting it where a track forks off right, just before a small parking area 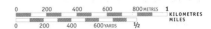.

Signed Tideswell Dale, the path follows a twisting, babbling brook, first on one bank and then crossing a little higher up. The dale is of a very different character to the others explored on the walk, well wooded and having a very gentle complexion. Towards the top, formal paths have been laid on both sides of the stream, rejoining to lead to a car park. Walk through and continue on a path parallel to the road beside a magnificent row of mature beech trees.

Continue at the edge of a field, leaving part way along through a gate on the right onto the road. Go left to find a path off right, just before a small water treatment plant **E**.

The path climbs to the right across the sloping hillside, shortly meeting a track. Walk right to reach a lane and drop back to the main road at the edge of the village. The church from which the walk began stands at the far end. ●

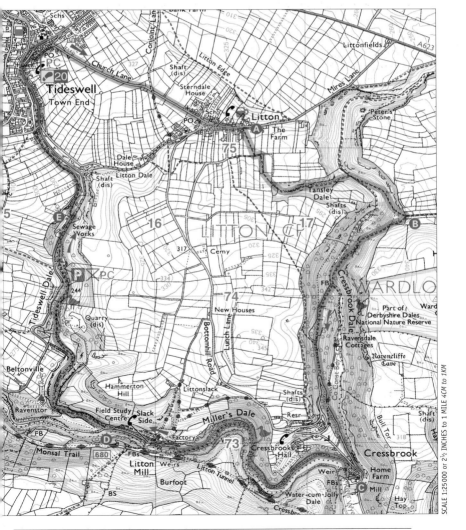

Three Shire Heads and Axe Edge Moor

		GPS waypoints
Start	Cat and Fiddle Inn	✎ SK 000 718
Distance	7¼ miles (11.7km)	Ⓐ SK 009 700
Height gain	1,080 feet (330m)	Ⓑ SK 009 685
Approximate time	3½ hours	Ⓒ SK 020 687
Parking	Roadside parking opposite pub	Ⓓ SK 026 703
Route terrain	Generally clear moorland paths, *care needed in mist*	Ⓔ SK 027 713
Ordnance Survey maps	Landranger 118 (Stoke-on-Trent & Macclesfield), Explorer OL24 (The Peak District – White Peak area)	

In poor weather, the moorland summit of the Macclesfield – Buxton road can appear bleak and uninviting, but a brighter complexion reveals panoramic views across a spacious landscape variously carpeted in heather and cotton grass. Meandering the remote folds and edges of Axe Edge Moor, the route leads to Three Shire Heads, a beautiful spot where streams and paths meet at an ancient packhorse bridge on which the counties of Cheshire, Staffordshire and Derbyshire converge.

At 1,690 feet (516m) the **Cat and Fiddle** is England's second highest inn, beaten only by the Tan Hill Inn in the northern Pennines. Built to serve the turnpike road, completed in 1823, the pub is enjoying a new lease of life as home to the country's highest distillery. The Forest Distillery is famous for both its whisky and gin, and in addition to its traditional hospitality, the inn now offers visitor tours and a shop.

✎ With your back to the inn, take the track opposite across open moorland. Beginning from such a high altitude there are immediately impressive views across the Cheshire plain while to the south-west, the distinctive peak of Shutlingsloe rises above Wildboarclough. After gently climbing, keep on with the

main track at a junction, signed to Three Shires Heads. It falls through Danebower Hollow, eventually meeting the main A54 Ⓐ. Walk right, doubling back after 200 yards along a gated track. In 100 yards, at the end of the accompanying fence, drop steeply past a lone chimney to a grassy path below. To the right it follows the meandering course of the infant River Dane, before long leading to a bridge across a side stream. Carry on along the valley for a further ¼ mile (400m) to a stone bridge across the Dane at Three Shire Heads Ⓑ.

It is a lovely spot at the confluence of confined, steep-sided and bracken-covered valleys, where two lively streams, each spanned by a narrow packhorse bridge, tumble over rocky

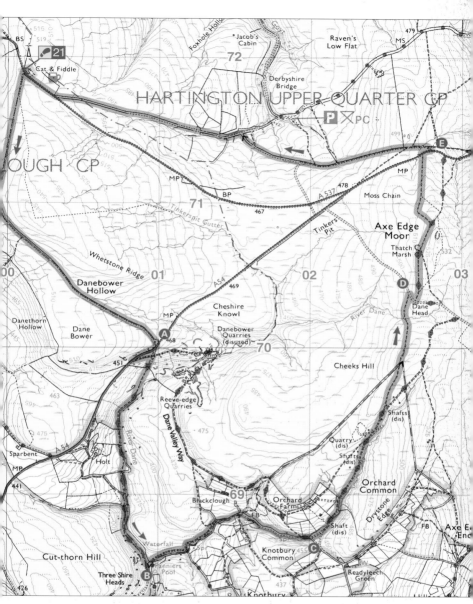

falls to mingle their waters. Just below is Panniers Pool, taking its name from the large baskets in which the pack animals carried their heavy loads. The place was perhaps the site of a ford before the bridges were built, or it may merely have been somewhere that the horses were taken down to the water to drink.

Turn over the first bridge and then walk ahead through a gate to gain height beside the tributary stream. Where the way later levels at a junction, bear left, sticking with the stream towards Orchard Common. Emerging

through a gate onto a tarmac track by the entrance to Black Clough Farm, keep ahead up the hill, before long reaching a right-hand bend . Fork left onto a track, which drops over a bridge before climbing away in a steady ascent. Go forward as the track bends to Orchard Farm, passing through a gate to continue on a broad path rising beside the clough. After ½ mile (800m), just beyond overgrown spoil heaps standing above to the left, look for a small concrete stump hidden in the grass on the right, which marks an abandoned mine shaft. There, bear left on a rising trod across the moor to the corner of a wall breaking the skyline. Crossing a stile, carry on in the same direction, eventually meeting a lane at Dane Head.

Go right, but then almost immediately swing left onto a broad grassy path that heads away across the stark expanses of Axe Edge Moor. To the east, the ground rises to over 1,800 feet (549m) before abruptly falling over the gritstone escarpment of Axe Edge, which overlooks Buxton as well as a good slice of the Peak District. The moor is a major watershed and five rivers; the Dove, Manifold, Wye, Derwent and Goyt, all begin their journey to the sea from its peaty slopes.

As the way crests, look for a narrower path splitting off on the left. It drops away before curving right, ultimately bringing you to the main A54 road. Cross right and double back left on a path beside a fence and broken wall. There are fine views to the right into the head of the Goyt Valley, while to the front, at the top of the hill is the **Cat and Fiddle Inn**. Meeting the corner of a lane, keep going into the valley. At the bottom, turn left and climb once more back to the main road, joining it just short of your starting point.

Across Axe Edge Moor to the Goyt Valley

Hathersage

Start	Hathersage	**GPS waypoints**	
Distance	7¼ miles (11.7km)	✎ SK 231 813	
Height gain	1,400 feet (425m)	Ⓐ SK 229 811	
Approximate time	3½ hours	Ⓑ SK 233 806	
Parking	Car park in Oddfellows Road – Pay and Display	Ⓒ SK 213 811	
		Ⓓ SK 221 817	
		Ⓔ SK 225 823	
Route terrain	Clear tracks and field paths, stepping stones across the River Derwent	Ⓕ SK 218 829	
		Ⓖ SK 229 837	
Dog friendly	Stepping stones may pose a problem for some dogs		
Ordnance Survey maps	Landranger 110 (Sheffield & Huddersfield), Explorer OL1 (The Peak District – Dark Peak area)		

In contrast to the high moorland, the Derwent Valley here is a mixture of green meadows, wooded valleys and rolling hills. The walk climbs for the views on both sides of the river before returning along the picturesque valley of Hood Brook. Note: Heavy rain can make the stepping stones across the River Derwent north of Offerton impassable and necessitate a riverside return to Leadmill Bridge to pick up the alternative route from Hathersage.

Today's picture of bright streets and attractive cottages is a far cry from the pall of 19th-century grime and smoke, when Hathersage's mills churned out millions of needles and pins. The village is, however, more famous for its literary connections, one real and the other legendary. Charlotte Brontë stayed here awhile, taking the name for her most famous heroine from tombs in the 14th-century church, Eyre. Little John, right-hand man of Robin Hood, is supposedly buried in the same graveyard, which is passed at the end of the walk.

✎ From the car park, follow Oddfellows Road to the right past the Memorial Hall and go left at the junction. Before reaching the railway, turn right into Dore Lane, continuing beyond the bridge to a bend in front of Nether Hall Lodge Ⓐ. Through a field-gate on the left, a farm track is signed away at the field edge to Leadmill Bridge. Emerging onto the road there, cross the bridge and immediately leave through a narrow gate on the right onto the riverbank Ⓑ.

Head upstream beside the Derwent. However, after 200 yards, bear left by a dilapidated barn to climb a wooded bank to a wall stile at the top. Follow the right-hand boundary into the next field, but where the wall later drops away, strike across to a gate onto a track below Mount Pleasant Farm. Pause to enjoy the view across to Stanage Edge and then take the track

Stepping across the Derwent

on the right towards Broadhay Farm. Straight after a bridge spanning Dunge Brook (a contraction of the old English 'dene ge' meaning valley district), leave through a gate on the left and walk upfield above the beck. Continue through another gate into Callow Wood, the ongoing path gaining height through the trees along the valley side. Eventually, pass out through a gate in the right-hand wall and bear left up the field to a stile. Just above is a gate into the yard of Callow House Farm.

Leave to the left, but then immediately cross a stile on the right to find a path doubling back above the former barns. Over another stile and stream, the obvious path continues across the hillside, shortly emerging onto a tarmac drive. To the right, it leads to Offerton Hall, one of seven large farmhouses in the area said to have been provided in the 14th century by Robert and Elizabeth Eyre for their

seven sons. Nearing the hall, the way twists abruptly down hill, passing its entrance and then a neighbouring cottage. Just past there, leave the drive through a field-gate on the right **C**.

A contained path drops through the field and continues as a downhill trod to the River Derwent where, if, the water level permits, cross the stepping stones.

Otherwise, follow the riverbank downstream back to Leadmill Bridge. Retrace your steps to Nether Hall lodge **A***, but now take the lane opposite and at the end, go left to the main road. Cross and turn right to find a path signed off between the bank and an outdoor shop, which continues behind house gardens and beside a cricket field. Rejoining the stream, keep going to a bridge. Cross and strike a diagonal course over parkland to rise through Cliff Wood. Emerging above the trees, accompany a fence up to Birley Farm. Over a stile behind the barns, go right and then left, leaving through gates* *onto a lane. Follow it left to a junction*  **E**, *there turning right to rejoin the main route.*

Assuming you made it across the river, head directly away, passing through gaps in old hedges to reach the main road. Follow it right for 200 yards then fork left up Hill Foot. A short distance beyond the railway bridge, look for a stepped path beside a cottage on the left **D**.

Climb to a hand-gate and on up a track. Where that swings right, cross the stile in front. Continue at the field edge to another stile and then keep right to a small gate. Now strike out across a final field to a squeeze gap onto a lane. Go

Little John's Grave

left up the hill to a junction **E**, there keeping left on Coggers Lane. In the 18th century Geer Green School stood in the adjacent field and was used by Charlotte Brontë as the model for Moreton School in her novel, *Jane Eyre*.

Carry on a further 150 yards then bear left through a gate into the corner of a field. Head out, with the trees of an old boundary on your right. Through a gate at the end, drop beside the left boundary to a stream at the bottom. Follow the ongoing hedge up to a gate, emerging at a junction of tracks by Nether Hurst. Take the one opposite, winding past a pond and bunkhouse. Where the track finishes, keep ahead on a sunken, hedged path, which leads to another old track, Hurstclough Lane **F**.

Follow it or the adjacent field path right for almost $^1/_2$ mile (800m) to a sharp right-hand bend, where there is a stile on the left. Climb beside a small stream, bearing right in the fourth field to find a stone stile in the corner. Strike across a final field to meet a lane opposite a house, Out Lane. Go right and then quickly left along a track beside the buildings, which continues over a cattle-grid across the fields. It eventually wanders down to a large farm, Green's House, entering a narrow yard between the buildings. Immediately through a gate at the far side, slip through a gap in the right-hand wall **G**.

Carry on down the fields towards a wood, dropping through the trees and over a bridge to continue beside Hood Brook. Emerging in a field, walk at the edge to reach a narrow lane.

Through a gate opposite, skirt Brookfield Manor and head across the field beyond. At a waymark in the middle, bear right along a track that continues across the next field. Through a gate at the far side, turn off to follow the hedge on the left. Over a stile and with the hedge now on your right, keep going in subsequent fields, the way cresting a low rise before falling to a stream. A stepped path scales the opposite bank; at the top of which go right to come out opposite the church. Walk left to enter the churchyard, where you will find Little John's grave opposite the south porch.

The band of Sherwood outlaws might be merely folk heroes, but when the burial here was opened in 1784, a huge thighbone was found, suggesting a man about 7 feet (2.13m) tall.

Continue west past the church and extension cemetery, leaving at the far end along a descending path to a lane. Go left to the main road and cross to a foot-path between the buildings opposite. Joining a street, walk ahead back to the car park. ●

Lantern Pike

		GPS waypoints	
Start	Hayfield		SK 036 869
Distance	7¼ miles (11.7km)	Ⓐ	SK 040 868
Height gain	1,400 feet (425m)	Ⓑ	SK 049 883
Approximate time	3½ hours	Ⓒ	SK 035 894
Parking	Car park at former railway station – Pay and Display	Ⓓ	SK 032 902
		Ⓔ	SK 029 904
Route terrain	Clear paths and tracks across moorland	Ⓕ	SK 023 895
		Ⓖ	SK 025 881
Ordnance Survey maps	Landranger 110 (Sheffield & Huddersfield), Explorer OL1 (The Peak District – Dark Peak area)	Ⓗ	SK 021 868

Nestling below the bleak upland of Kinder, Hayfield is the starting point for this grand circuit that encircles one of the head valleys of the River Sett. The prominent, local landmark of Lantern Pike offers expansive views before an easy valley return along the course of a disused railway.

Annual sheep dog trials, well dressing and a May Queen procession emphasise the village feel of Hayfield today. Yet during the 19th century, it had grown to a small but bustling town with the railway, which arrived in 1868, serving local industries such as textile mills and calico printing, paper-making and quarrying. Earlier, it had been a staging post on a packhorse trail across the hills, a fact remembered in the **Pack Horse Inn**, which has stood there since 1577. Many of the stone cottages date from the 17th century and were well-fenestrated in their upper storeys to admit light for weaving woollen cloth on hand-looms. More recently, Hayfield saw the birth of Arthur Lowe, remembered for, among many other things, his role as Captain Mainwaring in the ever-popular *Dad's Army* television series. The television theme is continued in the higher valley at Little Hayfield, where Tony Warren creator of *Coronation Street* and Pat Phoenix (Elsie Tanner), one of its original, long-standing stars both lived.

Begin from the car park at the former station and cross the main road

Birch Vale Reservoir

at the traffic lights. Carry on beside the church into the town centre and go left over the River Sett. Just beyond, turn right into Bank Street and continue along Kinder Road, which rises steeply out of the town. After ¼ mile (400m), as the gradient eases, look for a track signed off on the left to the **Snake Inn** Ⓐ.

The gated, stony track winds determinedly up the hillside, later climbing past a clump of beech trees, conspicuous by their isolation. Out to the left across the valley is Lantern Pike, over which the walk returns. Levelling, the path progresses onto the rougher, open moor and the National Trust access land. The scene opens ahead across the heather to Leygatehead Moor and farther right, the foreboding mass of Kinder Scout. Carry on for ¼ mile (400m) towards white-painted shooting cabins, to find a junction just before them Ⓑ.

Take the left path, signed to Glossop via Carr Meadow, which, beyond a short causeway over boggy ground, winds carelessly across the heath. Later dip to ford a brook and continue around the flank of The Knott, from where there is a superb view along the Sett Valley. The path then gradually steepens towards Carr Meadows, dropping to bridge a stream in Hollingworth Clough and meeting a track coming from the road Ⓒ.

Bearing right, climb at the edge of the open moor, taking the left branch when you reach a fork. The way now levels towards the head of the valley. Keep right where the path subsequently splits, continuing to a stile in the corner, which leads out to the road facing a junction Ⓓ.

The onward route lies along the lane opposite, signed towards Charlesworth. After ¼ mile (400m), just beyond the

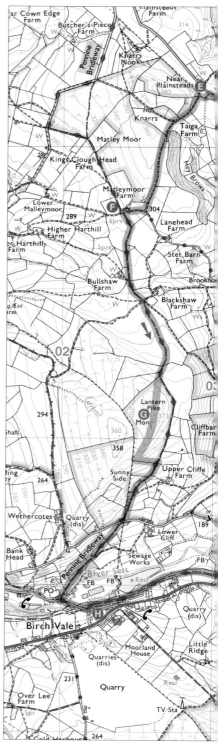

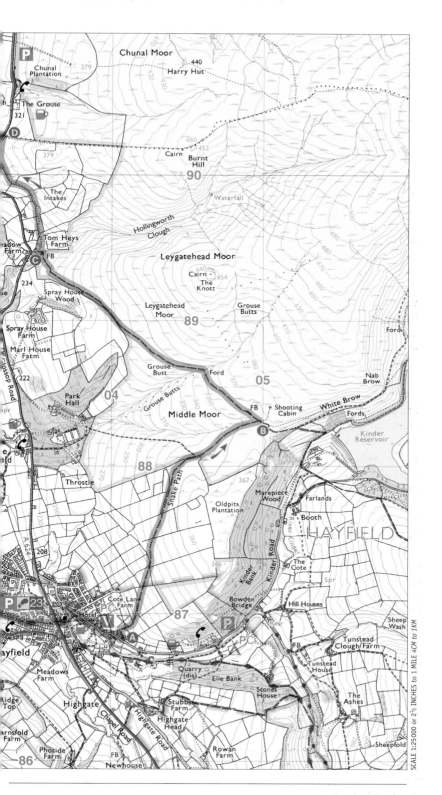

SCALE 1:25000 or 2½ INCHES to 1 MILE 4CM to 1KM

crest of the rise, leave along a way-marked track on the left **E**. Reaching a junction, bear left and, through a gate at the end, carry on at the edge of coarse pasture. Remain by the wall to find a stile in the corner and walk down to a gravel track. Turning right soon brings you to a junction by Matleymoor Farm **F**.

Take the walled track to the left, which leads towards Blackshaw Farm. As the track swings into the yard, go through a field-gate on the right into a rough, open pasture. Strike a diagonal left from the corner, soon picking up a trod making for Lantern Pike. Joining a track at the far side, follow it right through a gate and up onto the access land. Just beyond the National Trust sign, bear off right to make a direct ascent of the hill. The strenuous pull leads to a topograph on the summit **G**.

The way continues above a low but none the less impressive escarpment before descending to a wall. Turn left and follow it steeply down to regain the track you left earlier. To the right, through a gate, carry on down the hill, eventually emerging onto a narrow lane. Go briefly right past a row of one-time quarrymen's cottages before branching left along another downward track marked as the Pennine Bridleway to Hayfield. At a hairpin bend, keep ahead through a gate along an old, leafy way, which comes out beside mill cottages at Spinner Bottom below Birch Vale.

Turn left, crossing the River Sett to find, just past the **Sett Valley Café**, a waymarked path leaving through a gate on the left **H**. After a couple of twists it settles along the course of the former railway, heading up the valley above a large reservoir built to supply the mill. One mile's (1.6km) easy walking returns you to the car park. ●

On Lantern Pike

Wolfescote Dale

Beresford and Wolfscote Dales

Start	Hartington
Distance	8 miles (12.9km)
Height gain	1,360 feet (415m)
Approximate time	4 hours
Parking	In village
Route terrain	Paths, tracks and field trods, steep grassy descent
Ordnance Survey maps	Landranger 119 (Buxton & Matlock), Explorer OL24 (The Peak District – White Peak area)

GPS waypoints

- 🖉 SK 128 604
- Ⓐ SK 128 586
- Ⓑ SK 126 576
- Ⓒ SK 126 566
- Ⓓ SK 126 564
- Ⓔ SK 134 556
- Ⓕ SK 145 561
- Ⓖ SK 130 584
- Ⓗ SK 133 596

After its wide valley north of Hartington, the River Dove flows through the gorge-like Beresford and Wolfscote dales. Many declare these dales to be as equally attractive as Dovedale proper and this superlatively beautiful ramble includes two of the loveliest Peak District villages, some sweeping views and long stretches of glorious riverside walking through the dales themselves.

Like a number of Peak villages, Hartington was once a bustling centre, and the limestone houses, inns and shops grouped attractively around the spacious market place have the atmosphere more of a small town than a village. Dominated by a large and handsome medieval church, the village occupies a grand setting about ¹⁄₂ mile from the river above its narrowing into Beresford Dale.

🖉 From the market place, take the B5054 road towards Warslow, leaving left after some 150 yards for a footpath between **Hartington Farm Shop and Café** and the public conveniences, set back from the road. Signed to Beresford and Wolfscote Dales, it leads to a field behind, swinging right past a cottage and on by a wall. Through a gate, cross a track into the next field, the view

ahead inviting you into a lush and gentle wooded landscape. Slipping through a gap in a wall, maintain your direction and, beyond a gate, skirt the base of a low, conical hill. The way continues through a small wood to emerge beside the River Dove. The area is associated with the famous angler Izaak Walton, who wrote *The Compleat Angler* in 1676. He frequently fished this part of the river in the company of his friend Charles Cotton, who lived at nearby Beresford Hall. The hall was demolished in 1858, but the 17th-century 'fishing temple' survives. The path shortly crosses a footbridge by Pike Pool, so called by Charles Cotton, not for the fish but after the thin spire

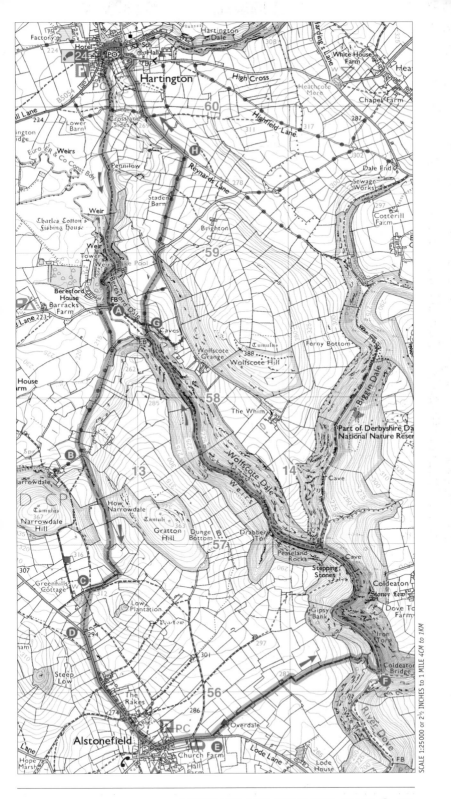

SCALE 1:25000 or 2½ INCHES to 1 MILE 4CM to 1KM

Above Alstonefield

of rock that towers above the river. Carry on through Beresford Dale, ignoring a second bridge at its end to turn out onto the end of a lane **A**.

Walk from the river, but after 50 yards turn left through a gate. Signed as a cycle route to Hartington, the track hugs the field edge. Keep ahead where the cycle path later leaves left, continuing through a succession of gates for almost ¾ mile (1.2km) and eventually rising to a sharp right turn **B**. Go forward through a gate along a gently rising grassy fold, appropriately called Narrowdale, and carry on beyond another gate, joining a wall on your right into the broader upper valley. Shortly pick up another wall on your left, pausing at the top corner to enjoy the retrospective view before turning right to a gate and stile. Follow a walled track over the crest, shortly reaching an intersecting path indicated by a four-way signpost **C**. Pass through the kissing-gate on the left and, guided by a sign to Alstonefield, bear right across the pasture to another gate at the corner of a small wood. Maintain the diagonal across the resultant fields to emerge onto a lane **D**.

Turn left into Alstonefield, a delightfully unspoiled and peaceful village standing 900 feet (274m) on a plateau between the Dove and Manifold valleys. Grey stone cottages are grouped around a charming green and village inn, while its lovely old church can be found along a lane, just to the south. Although dating mostly from the 14th and 15th centuries, it retains a Norman doorway and chancel arch and contains the family pew formerly used by the Cottons from nearby Beresford Hall.

Approaching the village centre go left and then left again at successive junctions, following signs to Lode Mill and Ashbourne. After ¼ mile (400m) turn off along the second of two tracks on the left, signed to the Youth Hostel and Coldeaton Bridge via Gipsy Bank **E**. It later doglegs right and left, becoming narrower and ultimately ending at a stile. The onward path drops right to the head of a shallow gully, following it sharply down to Coldeaton Bridge spanning the River Dove below **F**.

Cross the bridge and turn left, accompanying the river through Wolfscote Dale, a sinuous steep-sided gorge, thickly wooded at first, but later opening to smooth grassy slopes broken by spectacular limestone crags. Keep going for almost 2 miles (3.2km) past Gipsy Bank Bridge to Frank i' th' Rocks Bridge **G**. Remaining on this bank, leave the river along an uphill track, continuing across a junction to a right-hand bend at the top of the hill. Go forward over a stile and bear right, crossing the field to a wall stile somewhat short of the far corner. *(Note that between April and July, you are asked to divert around the perimeter track to the lane.)* Joining the lane, follow it left and around a bend, leaving soon after along a track signed left to Hartington. Very shortly swinging right, it falls in a straight gentle descent to Reynards Lane **H**. Walk down the hill towards the village, going left and left again when you reach the main road to return to the market place. ●

Macclesfield Forest and the 'Cheshire Matterhorn'

		GPS waypoints
Start	Wildboarclough	✐ SJ 986 699
Distance	7¾ miles (12.5km)	**A** SJ 981 713
Height gain	1,770 feet (540m)	**B** SJ 985 719
Approximate time	4 hours	**C** SJ 979 722
Parking	Car park at Clough House	**D** SJ 971 722
Route terrain	Upland pasture and forest paths, a steep initial descent off Shutlingsloe	**E** SJ 962 726
		F SJ 952 715
		G SJ 956 710
		H SJ 976 695
Ordnance Survey maps	Landranger 118 (Stoke-on-Trent & Macclesfield), Explorer OL24 (The Peak District – White Peak area)	**J** SJ 982 690

From a distance it is easy to see why Shutlingsloe has been described as the 'Cheshire Matterhorn', for although only rising to 1,659 feet (517m), its abrupt and distinctive peak bears a striking resemblance to its Continental counterpart. Much of this ramble is across the former royal hunting domain of Macclesfield Forest, a sparsely populated area of isolated farms, rolling hills, wild moorlands and rushing streams. The area has seen little change over the centuries, apart from the planting of conifers and the construction of reservoirs on its western perimeter. For most of the way this is an undulating route but towards the end there is a long, though not particularly steep or strenuous climb to the summit of Shutlingsloe, followed by a short, sharp descent.

Macclesfield Forest comprises a number of plantations occupying the western slopes of the Peak District overlooking the Cheshire plain. It is just a small part of what, in the Middle Ages, was a large, royal hunting forest, much of which would have been as it is today, open moorland rather than thick woodland.

✐ From the northern end of the car park, turn right along the lane. After a mile (1.6km), just past a turning to Forest Chapel, leave along a farm track on the right **A**. Over a stream, but before a cattle-grid, go left onto another track rising beside Clough Brook. Reaching a cottage and barns at the end, wend left through a gate to a bridge spanning the stream. Continue briefly along the opposite bank of the stream, before moving left through an open gateway **B**, from which a contained broad grass track swings left up the hill.

After gaining height beside a ruined building and old walls, it veers right past a stepped stile on the left. Cross that and strike right up the hillside to another stile beside a gate at the top corner. Beyond, follow a descending wall. Approaching the corner, look for a stone stile and cross to continue down on the other flank of the wall. Pass through a gate at the bottom corner and carry on to a bridge over a stream. Bear left up to a gate onto a lane beside the entrance to a house **C**.

Go left and then immediately right at a junction, the climbing lane signed to Forest Chapel. After some 100 yards, turn right onto an old, sunken track that rises over the hill to the chapel. This plain and simple church, built in 1673 and reconstructed in 1831, is in total harmony with the surroundings. The church is one of several where a rush-bearing ceremony is held to commemorate the annual renewal of the rushes that originally covered most church floors.

At a junction just past the church, take a track on the right, which soon leads to the edge of a forest plantation **D**. Leave the track through a gate on the left from which a clear path winds away among the trees. After $\frac{1}{2}$ mile (800m), the way falls more steeply to reach a junction in a partial clearing before a ruined barn **E**.

Signed to Langley, the track left resumes an easy descent through the forest. Eventually joining a tarmac lane, the more open ground to the right affords a view to the bold crags of Tegg's Nose. Carry on to a junction in front of a pub, **Leather's Smithy F**.

Immediately past the merging lane, leave through a squeeze gap beside a gate on the left, onto a gravel track

below Ridgegate Reservoir. At a fork on the far side, bear left towards Shutlingsloe, dipping to cross another dam. Keeping right, climb away from the water. Swinging left at the top, follow a track out to the corner of a lane. Walk ahead a little way to find a gated entrance to the forest on the right **G**.

Instead of taking the main bridlepath, go through a small gate to its left from which a footpath is signed to Trentabank. After briefly shadowing the lane, it weaves down a wooded bank to meet a main forest track. Cross to the narrower path directly opposite. It winds up into the trees and before long meets another broad track. Picking up signs to Shutlingsloe once more, go right and then keep left when you meet another track. Reaching a junction in front of a gate, walk right, the way resuming a steady climb. Beyond

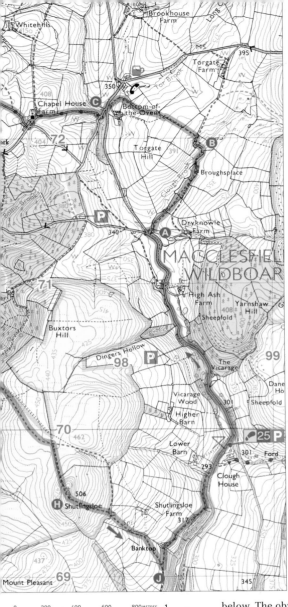

dramatically into view. Through a gate, turn beside the wall towards Shutlingsloe, soon crossing a stile for the final pull to the summit **H**.

Standing apart from the main body of hills, the spot affords a magnificent panorama on a clear day. To the north-west is Macclesfield Forest and Tegg's Nose, while to the west the land falls away to the Cheshire plain. To the south are the Roaches above the Tittesworth Reservoir, while to the east the ground rises to the bleak expanse of Axe Edge Moor.

The route off is waymarked just beyond the trig point, a rocky path dropping steeply down the craggy face. Those with short legs will find the first section a bit of a scramble, but the gradient soon eases as the descent continues on the grass below. The obvious path lies over a couple of stiles before crossing a stream to join a tarmac drive. Follow it to the right, shortly reaching a cattle-grid **J**.

Double back left on a track above a wood, passing a cottage and barn to carry on along a grass path beside a wall. The way continues generally ahead over stiles and a small stream, finally ending at a lane. Follow it left back to the car park at Clough House. ●

another gate, ignore the first right, a bridleway, and continue a little farther to find a path signed off right to Shutlingsloe. Rising to a kissing-gate, leave the forest and carry on along a flagged path that gains height across the open hillside. As the way briefly levels, the distinctive peak comes

Derwent Edge

		GPS waypoints
Start	Fairholmes National Park Centre	☑ SK 172 893
Distance	9 miles (14.5km)	Ⓐ SK 173 896
Height gain	1,600 feet (490m)	Ⓑ SK 170 919
Approximate time	4½ hours	Ⓒ SK 176 911
Parking	Car park at start – Pay and Display	Ⓓ SK 193 912
Route terrain	Clear moorland paths, *take care in mist*	Ⓔ SK 197 909
		Ⓕ SK 203 880
Ordnance Survey maps	Landranger 110 (Sheffield & Huddersfield), Explorer OL1 (The Peak District – Dark Peak area)	Ⓖ SK 187 884

From just below the massive wall of the Derwent Dam, the route hugs the shore of the Derwent Reservoir before climbing across fresh and bracing moorland to the prominent outcrop of Back Tor on Derwent Edge. There follows a superb scenic walk along the edge from where many of the best-known landmarks in the northern Peak District can be picked out, before descending to the Ladybower Reservoir. The forested slopes above the long tongues of water filling the Derwent Valley are a foil to the wild moors above and lend much charm to this striking landscape.

Towards the end of the 19th century, there was pressure to improve water supplies to the rapidly growing cities of Derby, Nottingham, Leicester and Sheffield. The upper Derwent Valley was an obvious choice for a vast reservoir, sparsely populated and relatively narrow, which facilitated the construction of the dam, and with a catchment that enjoyed (if that is the right word) a high annual rainfall. In time two more dams were built, forming a chain of reservoirs: Howden, Derwent and Ladybower, creating one of the largest man-made areas of water in Europe.

🔲 A path signed to the dams leaves the car park by the National Park Visitor Centre. Joining the lane, follow it right to sweep below the high wall. Because of the geographical similarities between the Derwent Reservoir and the Möhne and Eder dams in the Ruhr, the RAF used the valley to practise for the famous Dambusters' raid in 1943, the subsequent film adopting the very same location. There is a memorial to those who lost their lives during the raid on the west side of the dam. Just beyond the bend, abandon the lane for the second of two paths that double back left Ⓐ. Signed 'Derwent Dam East Tower' it slants uphill through a conifer plantation, and passes the top of the dam wall to join a service track.

Follow it above the shore for almost 1½ miles (2.4km) towards the Howden Dam at the top end of the lake. As the trail then gently falls beside an embankment to the foot of Abbey Brook, look for a path signed off to

Ewden via Broomhead for Bradfield and Strines **B**. Almost immediately, turn off sharp right to rise obliquely across the steep slope of Abbey Bank, leaving the plantation through a gate to continue beside a hollow way. After briefly

turning more directly up the hill, carry on above a broken wall. Maintain your height where the wall subsequently falls away, walking on to a crossing of paths by a low cairn **C**. Take the path off left to Strines and Foulstone.

Higher up, the path curves to the right, following a broken wall, and eventually reaching a stile beside a gate and

signpost. Still making for Strines over a heathery moor, your immediate objective, Lost Lad, is now clear ahead. Keep left at a later unsigned fork, the path soon curving right. Remain with the main trail as it rises beside an old ditch and embankment boundary, becoming stepped and flagged before a final assault on the summit of Lost Lad **D**.

The prominent outcrop is named after a young shepherd boy who, beset by weather on the moor had become disoriented. As he lay on the hilltop dying from exposure, he carved the words 'lost lad' on a boulder. In good conditions, however, this is a grand spot and a topograph helps identify some of the features that can be seen. Carry on over the top, dipping before climbing once more to Back Tor on the ridge in front of you. To gain the summit trig point **E** involves a scramble, but the view all around is something quite splendid.

The onward path curves to the right along the broad undulating spine of Derwent Edge, shortly passing a stone pillar that marks a crossing path to

Bradfield Gate. Stick with the paved path along the edge, where the outcropping gritstone has been weathered into some weird and wonderful shapes. Encountered in slow succession are the 'Cakes of Bread', Dovestone Tor, the 'Salt Cellar', White Tor and finally the 'Wheel Stones', also known as the 'Coach and Horses'. Beyond there, the path gently loses height for another $^{1}/_{4}$ mile (400m) before reaching a junction of paths marked by a signpost **F**.

Take the path right, marked to Derwent, which falls steadily to meet a lower path beside a wall. A little way to the right, fork left through a gate in the wall, further descending towards the right-hand corner of a forest plantation. Through another gate carry on at the edge of the trees, shortly entering the National Trust estate surrounding High House Farm. Continue down to a group of restored 17th-century barns, the path winding between them to leave through the smaller of the two gates. A paved way drops beside a pretty clough, curving away towards the bottom to end at a track **G**.

Back Tor

Follow it to the right above the Ladybower Reservoir, soon reaching a bridge across Mill Brook. Beneath the waters of the reservoir at this point lies the submerged village of Derwent, which was drowned by the rising waters in 1943 when the dam was completed. Carry on along the lane for a further $1^{1}/_{4}$ miles (2km), eventually passing beneath the Derwent dam to return to the car park. ●

Edale and Jacob's Ladder

		GPS waypoints	
Start	Edale	✎	SK 123 853
Distance	8 miles (12.9km)	**A**	SK 122 861
Height gain	1,690 feet (515m)	**B**	SK 105 872
Approximate time	4 hours	**C**	SK 095 872
Parking	Car park below village – Pay and Display	**D**	SK 079 865
Route terrain	Moorland paths, easy scramble onto moor, *take care in mist*	**E**	SK 081 861
Ordnance Survey maps	Landranger 110 (Sheffield & Huddersfield), Explorer OL1 (The Peak District – Dark Peak area)	**F**	SK 102 852

This walk starts from the hamlet of Edale and rises gently at first, up the spectacular valley of Grindsbrook Clough and eventually scrambling out at the top onto the southern flank of the remote Kinder Scout plateau above the Vale of Edale. There are some splendid views and a sense of wilderness as the next stage skirts the head of the dale, passing some fantastically shaped gritstone boulders. After descending Jacob's Ladder there is an easy final stretch across the valley fields.

Strictly speaking, Edale is the name of a valley in which lie five distinct hamlets or booths, although in practice, the name has become identified with the main settlement, Grindsbrook Booth. To the north stretches the highest and wildest moorland of the Dark Peak and Edale has become a major walking centre. It is also the start (or finish) of the Pennine Way, which traverses some of England's remotest countryside on its 250-mile (400km) route to Kirk Yetholme in the Cheviot Hills on the Scottish border.

✎ Leaving the car park by the toilets, go right beneath the railway and follow the lane to **The Old Nag's Head** at the top of the village. Beyond there, it degrades to a track leading to a stone lodge at the entrance of Grindslow House **A**. Turn off there along a path on the right over a bridge, signed to Grindsbrook.

To the left a flagged path rises gently across an open hillside field, before long entering a pleasant wood. Emerging at the far side, cross a stream and continue up the narrowing valley, the way steadily becoming more rugged. Higher up, path and stream come together, the path eventually forced to pick a better line above the opposite bank. Where the valley then splits, keep with the left branch, scrambling on to emerge below a large cairn at the head of Grindsbrook Clough **B**. Ignoring the path off sharp left, instead bear left to follow a slabbed path striking west, which crosses the shoulder of Grindslow Knoll to continue above the edge of Crowden Clough. You are following the perimeter of the vast expanse of Kinder Scout; a bleak, featureless waste furrowed by deep peat

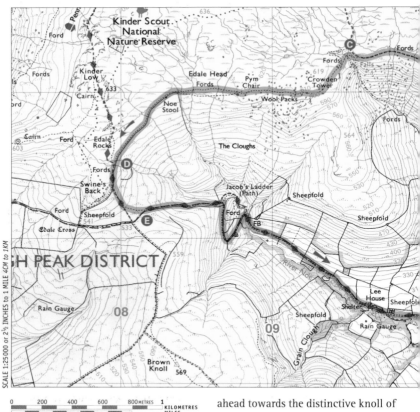

gullies known as groughs. The views to the south extend across the whole of the White Peak, the prominent hill to the east across the valley being Lose Hill. Intermittently paved, the way remains clear, eventually leading you to the head of Crowden Brook **C**.

Cross the brook below its tributary streams and climb towards a great buttress of rock, Crowden Tower. The way winds on past the ever-more fantastic gritstone rock formations of the Wool Packs and Pym Chair. Beyond, the going can be boggy as it crosses the gathering grounds of the River Noe to reach the last outcrop, Noe Stool. Curving around the head of the valley, stay below Edale Rocks to join the Pennine Way at a large cairn **D**. Walk

ahead towards the distinctive knoll of Swine's Back, keeping with the paved path as it then curves left to meet a track beside a dilapidated stone wall **E**.

Follow it down to the left, shortly reaching a junction by a cairn. Either path will do, that to the left is short and steep, the one through the gate finds an easier line in an extended loop. Both lead to a narrow stone bridge across the infant Noe. Known as Jacob's Ladder, the path once formed part of a major packhorse route across the moors. From the bridge it is then easy walking along the valley to Lee Farm, the way becoming a metalled track as it approaches Upper Booth. Opposite a telephone box **F**, a fingerpost to Edale directs you left into the farmyard. Passing a barn go right and then almost immediately left, turning right again after a few paces through a gate along a

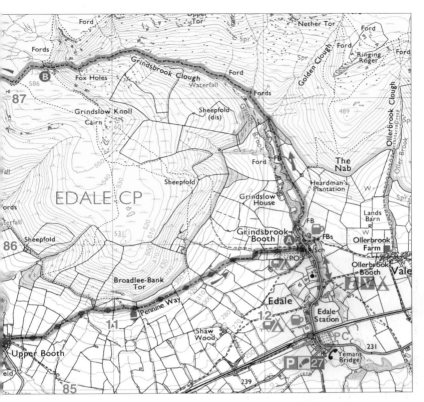

track, still signed to Edale. Beyond another gate, the way lies as an obvious trod across successive fields, shortly passing a ruined barn to a small gate. The main path winds on through an area of hummocky ground, crossing more fields before leaving through a final gate. To the right, an old narrow track bordered by hawthorn, ash and holly follows a stream back to the head of the village by **The Old Nag's Head**. Return along the lane to the car park. ●

Among Wool Packs

Lathkill Dale

		GPS waypoints
Start	Monyash	
Distance	10½ miles (16.9km), shorter version 8½ miles (13.7km)	SK 149 666
		Ⓐ SK 172 653
		Ⓑ SK 192 644
Height gain	1,600 feet (490m)	Ⓒ SK 197 648
Approximate time	5 hours, shorter version 4 hours	Ⓓ SK 202 661
Parking	Car park in village	Ⓔ SK 212 656
Route terrain	Generally good, but occasionally rocky paths. *Note: the route through Lathkill Dale between Ⓓ and Ⓕ follows a permissive path, which is closed on Wednesdays between November and January*	Ⓕ SK 183 657
		Ⓖ SK 174 655
Ordnance Survey maps	Landranger 119 (Buxton & Matlock), Explorer OL24 (The Peak District – White Peak area)	

The Derbyshire Dales are famed for their outstanding beauty and, by any criteria, Lathkill Dale is one of the loveliest as this walk so richly demonstrates. Starting from the attractive village of Monyash, the route crosses open country, briefly dipping through the valley to Over Haddon. It soon meanders to the foot of the dale at Conksbury Bridge, from which there is a superlatively beautiful 3½ mile (5.6km) ramble along the steep sided, wooded banks of the Lathkill, undoubtedly the highlight of the walk. Emerging through a rocky gorge at the head of the dale, it is then only a short stroll back to Monyash.

Monyash, a farming and former lead-mining village, sits high on the limestone uplands near the head of Lathkill Dale. A fine 14th-century church and the base of a market cross on the village green hint at the settlement's importance during medieval times, when it grew as a market at the focus of routes through the region.

🖉 From the car park, go right to the crossroads and then left past the **Bulls Head** pub. Turn into the churchyard and walk beside the church, leaving along a track beyond onto a lane. Follow it left to a bend and then keep ahead along a walled track, the Limestone Way. Take the left branch

where it subsequently forks.

Through a gate at the end, accompany the right-hand wall to a second squeeze stile and then strike a left diagonal across the neighbouring field. Beyond a gap stile in the middle of the wall, keep with the Limestone Way beside the wall. Approaching the corner of the second field, slip through a gate and continue in the adjacent enclosure. Emerging at the bottom, join a track down to One Ash Grange Farm. As suggested by the name, this was once a monastic grange.

Keep ahead past the first barns but then, watch for a waymark directing

Along the Limestone Way

you left behind the main buildings and past a line of restored pigsties. A little farther along is a larder or dairy store, set below the cool of an overhanging limestone slab. At a fork bear right and pass between a large corrugated shed and old stone barns to a stile. *Be careful, for there is a deep drop into the field beyond.* Go forward along a shallow depression, passing through a gate into the head of Cales Dale. Descend a steep rocky path into the gorge, briefly levelling along a shelf beneath a limestone cliff before turning right to a stile and fingerpost at the bottom **Ⓐ**.

Climb a stepped path to the field above and head to a kissing-gate at the far side, glancing back for a superb view into upper Lathkill Dale. Maintain your direction across the next two pastures, and then go left to a kissing-gate into a wood. Walk straight through and cross a small paddock into more trees. In the field beyond, go right to a gate and then strike a left diagonal to the far corner. Follow a path through the tip of Low Moor Plantation and keep the same line across the subsequent fields, a developing trod eventually guiding you to a gated stile, about halfway along the right-hand wall. Cross left to a second stile and walk the length of a final field, leaving onto a lane at the far corner **Ⓑ**.

Follow it left downhill for a little over ¼ mile (400m) before mounting a waymarked stile on the left **Ⓒ**. Bear right across the field, aiming for Over Haddon on the far hillside. Maintain the heading, eventually dropping towards a farm tucked into a fold. Skirt the corner of a wall as you approach, passing through a couple of gates into a large enclosure at the heart of the grange. Leave between the barns opposite to the field beyond, where a sign points half-right to Over Haddon. Through a gate in the corner, a track slopes steeply along the side of the Lathkill gorge, doubling back to a bridge across the river **Ⓓ**.

You can shorten the walk at this point by omitting the loop through Over

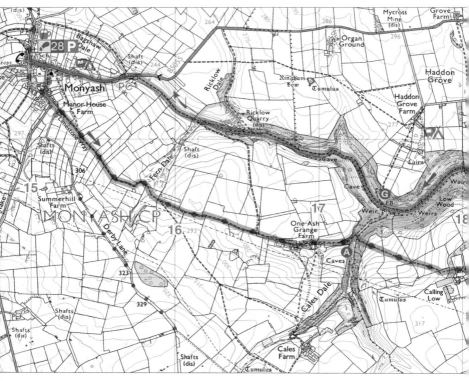

SCALE 1:26316 or 2½ INCHES to 1 MILE 3.8CM to 1KM

| 0 | 200 | 400 | 600 | 800 METRES | 1 |
| 0 | 200 | 400 | 600 YARDS | | ½ |

KILOMETRES
MILES

Haddon, in which case, a few paces up the lane ahead, turn off left along the valley path. (See note opposite.)

However, the opportunity for refreshment in the village and fine panoramic views across the lower dale make the additional 2 miles (3.2km) well worth the effort. Carry on up the lane into the village, bearing right at a junction along the main street. Strung along the hillside at some 800 feet (245m) above sea level, this remote community enjoys striking vistas across Lathkill Dale and the valleys of the Wye and Derwent. Over Haddon's present tranquility belies its industrial past, for, like many other similarly sleepy Peakland villages, it was once a lead-mining settlement.

Where the road then bends left, keep ahead on School Lane, passing a Wesleyan chapel to go behind the **Lathkil Hotel**. As the lane doubles back on itself, leave over a gated squeeze stile in the corner and bear right across the slope of the field to another stile in the far wall. Keep the same angle across the next field to a gate in the lower fence and walk on along the lip of the gorge. Entering another field, wend right above the bottom wall. Where it later kinks down, look for a stile partly hidden by ivy and drop to a small parking area below. Follow the lane down to Conksbury Bridge, turning off right just before it onto a path beside the river **E**.

For the next 3½ miles (5.6km), the walk winds beside the river through the exceptionally beautiful Lathkill Dale. The character of the valley is constantly changing, from lush woodland rich in wild flowers and harbouring many

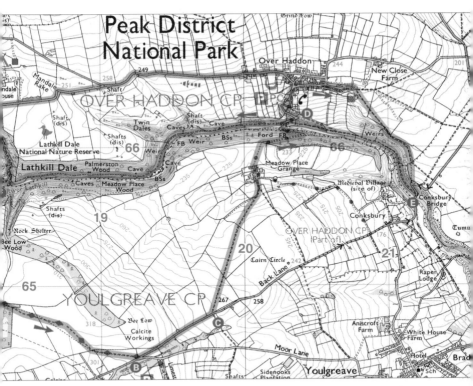

small birds at this end to a Spartan rocky gorge at the other. The river is crystal clear and supports a wide range of plants, insects and fish, and the water birds that feed upon them. Prolonged good weather can make the river disappear, although the water still flows deep underground, seeping through a maze of natural caves and old mine workings. Reaching Lathkill Lodge, where you first crossed the river **D**, turn up the lane as before, but almost immediately, leave through a gate to continue on a permissive riverside path.

*Note: should the path be closed, the detour from Point **D** is via Over Haddon and along the lane west. Keep ahead at a fork and continue for a further $^1/_2$ mile (800m) before turning in at the entrance to Mill Farm. Walk between the buildings and out along a walled track that winds down a side dale to return to Lathkill Dale at Point **F**.*

A little farther along, a bridge provides access to the remains of Bateman's House; a miner's dwelling built on top of the shaft. Bring a torch for a ladder gives access to a chamber beneath, where a pump was installed to lift water from the mine. Return to the path and carry on up the valley, later emerging briefly from the woods to cross a small meadow at the mouth of a side dale. Notice a couple of discarded millstones beside the path just beyond there. Keep going, eventually passing a bridge across the river at the foot of Cales Dale **G**.

As you progress, the gorge narrows and before long, there is no water flowing over the bouldery streambed. Beyond the debris of a redundant quarry, the gorge opens to the head of the dale. Carry on along a slight grassy fold through a couple of fields, finally emerging onto a lane. Follow it left back into Monyash. ●

Further Information

 ## Safety on the Hills

The hills, mountains and moorlands of Britain, though of modest height compared with those in many other countries, need to be treated with respect. Friendly and inviting in good weather, they can quickly be transformed into wet, misty, windswept and potentially dangerous areas of wilderness in bad weather. Even on an outwardly fine and settled summer day, conditions can rapidly deteriorate at high altitudes and, in winter, even more so.

Therefore it is advisable always to take both warm and waterproof clothing, sufficient nourishing food, a hot drink, first-aid kit, torch and whistle. Wear suitable footwear, such as strong walking boots or shoes that give a good grip over rocky terrain and on slippery slopes. Try to obtain a local weather forecast and bear it in mind before you start. Do not be afraid to abandon your proposed route and return to your starting point in the event of a sudden and unexpected deterioration in the weather. Do not go alone and allow enough time to finish the walk well before nightfall.

Most of the walks described in this book do not venture into remote wilderness areas and will be safe to do, given due care and respect, at any time of year in all but the most unreasonable weather. Indeed, a crisp, fine winter day often provides perfect walking conditions, with firm ground underfoot and a clarity that is not possible to achieve in the other seasons of the year. A few walks, however, are suitable only for reasonably fit and experienced hill walkers able to use a compass and should definitely not be tackled by anyone else during the winter months or in bad weather, especially high winds and mist. These are indicated in the general description that precedes each of the walks.

 ## Walkers and the Law

The Countryside and Rights of Way Act (CRoW Act 2000) gives a public right of access in England and Wales to land mapped as open country (mountain, moor, heath and down) or registered common land. These areas are known as *open access land*, and include land around the coastline, known as *coastal margin*.

Where You Can Go
Rights of Way
Prior to the introduction of the CRoW Act, walkers could only legally access the countryside along public rights of way. These are either 'footpaths' (for walkers only) or 'bridleways' (for walkers, riders on horseback and pedal cyclists). A third category called 'Byways open to all traffic' (BOATs), is used by motorised vehicles as well as those using non-mechanised transport. Mainly they are green lanes, farm and estate roads, although occasionally they will be found crossing mountainous area.

Rights of way are marked on Ordnance Survey maps. Look for the green broken lines on the Explorer maps, or the red dashed lines on Landranger maps.

The term 'right of way' means exactly what it says. It gives a right of passage over what, for the most part, is private land. Under pre-CRoW legislation walkers were required to keep to the line of the right of way and not stray onto land on either side. If you did inadvertently wander off the right of way, either because of faulty map reading or because the route was not clearly indicated on the ground, you were technically trespassing.

Local authorities have a legal obligation to ensure that rights of way are kept clear and free of obstruction, and are signposted where they leave metalled roads. The duty of local authorities to install signposts extends to the placing of signs along a path or way, but only where the authority considers it necessary to have a signpost or waymark to assist persons unfamiliar with the locality.

CRoW Access Rights

Access Land

As well as being able to walk on existing rights of way, under CRoW legislation you have access to large areas of open land and, under further legislation, a right of coastal access, which is being implemented by Natural England, giving for the first time the right of access around all England's open coast. This includes plans for an England Coast Path (ECP) which will run for 2,795 miles (4,500 kilometres). A corresponding Wales Coast Path has been open since 2012.

Coastal access rights apply within the coastal margin (including along the ECP) unless the land falls into a category of excepted land or is subject to local restrictions, exclusions or diversions.

You can of course continue to use rights of way to cross access land, but you can lawfully leave the path and wander at will in these designated areas.

Where to Walk

Access Land is shown on Ordnance Survey Explorer maps by a light yellow tint surrounded by a pale orange border. New orange coloured 'i' symbols on the maps will show the location of permanent access information boards installed by the access authorities. Coastal Margin is shown on Ordnance Survey Explorer maps by a pink tint.

Restrictions

The right to walk on access land may lawfully be restricted by landowners, but whatever restrictions are put into place on access land they have no effect on existing rights of way, and you can continue to walk on them.

Dogs

Dogs can be taken on access land, but must be kept on leads of two metres or less between 1 March and 31 July, and at all times where they are near livestock. In addition landowners may impose a ban on all dogs from fields where lambing takes place for up to six weeks in any year. Dogs may be banned from moorland used for grouse shooting and breeding for up to five years.

General Obstructions

Obstructions can sometimes cause a problem on a walk and the most common of these is where the path across a field has been ploughed over. It is legal for a farmer to plough up a path provided that it is restored within two weeks. This does not always happen and you are faced with the dilemma of following the line of the path, even if this means treading on crops, or walking round the edge of the field. Although the latter course of action seems the most sensible, it does mean that you would be trespassing.

Other obstructions can vary from overhanging vegetation to wire fences across the path, locked gates or even a cattle feeder on the path.

Use common sense. If you can get round the obstruction without causing damage, do so. Otherwise only remove as much of the obstruction as is necessary to secure passage.

If the right of way is blocked and cannot be followed, there is a long-standing view that in such circumstances there is a right to deviate, but this cannot wholly be relied on. Although it is accepted in law that highways (and that includes rights of way) are for the public service, and if the usual track is impassable, it is for the general good that people should be entitled to pass into another line. However, this should not be taken as indicating a right to deviate whenever a way is impassable. If in doubt, retreat.

Report obstructions to the local authority and/or the Ramblers.

 Useful Organisations

Campaign to Protect Rural England
Tel. 020 7981 2800
www.cpre.org.uk

Camping and Caravanning Club
Site bookings Tel. 024 7647 5426
www.campingandcaravanningclub.co.uk

Campaign for National Parks
Tel. 020 7981 0890
www.cnp.org.uk

English Heritage
Tel. 0370 333 1181
www.english-heritage.org.uk

Forestry Commission
Tel. 0300 067 4567
www.forestry.gov.uk

Friends of the Peak District
Tel. 0114 279 2655
www.friendsofthepeak.org.uk

National Trust
Membership and general enquiries
Tel. 0344 800 1895
www.nationaltrust.org.uk
East Midlands Regional Office
Tel. 01909 486411

Natural England
Tel. 0300 060 3900
www.gov.uk/government/organisations/
natural-england

Ordnance Survey
Tel. 03456 05 05 05
www.ordnancesurvey.co.uk

Peak and Northern Footpaths Society
Tel. 0161 480 3565
www.peakandnorthern.org.uk

Peak District National Park Authority
Tel. 01629 816200
www.peakdistrict.gov.uk

Peak District Information Centres
Bakewell
Tel. 01629 816558
Castleton
Tel. 01629 816572
The Moorland Centre, Edale
Tel. 01443 670207
Upper Derwent
Tel. 01433 650953

Ramblers
Tel. 020 7339 8500
www.ramblers.org.uk

Visit Peak District & Derbyshire
www.visitpeakdistrict.com

Tourist information centres:
Ashbourne: Tel: 01335 343666
Bakewell: Tel: 01629 816558
Buxton: Tel: 01298 25106
Castleton: Tel: 01629 816572
Congleton: Tel: 01260 271095
Cromford: Tel: 01629 533298
Darley Dale: Tel: 01629 761103
Leek: Tel: 01538 395530
Macclesfield: Tel: 01625 378123
Manifold Valley: Tel: 01538 483741
Matlock: Tel: 01629 761103
Matlock Bath: Tel: 01629 583834
Saddleworth: Tel: 01457 874093
The Moorland Centre: Tel: 01433 670207
Upper Derwent Valley: Tel: 01433 650953

Youth Hostels Association
Tel. 01629 592700
www.yha.org.uk

 Ordnance Survey maps of the Peak District

The Peak District is covered by Ordnance Survey 1:50 000 scale (1¼ inches to 1 mile or 2cm to 1km) Landranger sheets 109, 110, 118 and 119. These all-purpose maps are packed with information to help you explore the area. Viewpoints, picnic sites, places of interest, caravan and camping sites are shown, as well as public rights of way information such as footpaths and bridleways.

To examine the Peak District in more detail, and especially if you are planning walks, Ordnance Survey Explorer Maps at 1:25 000 (2½ inches to 1 mile or 4cm to 1km) scale are ideal.

OL1 – The Peak District (Dark Peak area)
OL24 – The Peak District (White Peak area)
OL21 – South Pennines

Ordnance Survey maps and guides are available from most booksellers, stationers and newsagents.

Text: Dennis and Jan Kelsall
Photography: Dennis and Jan Kelsall. Front cover: © David Chapman/Alamy
                       Stock Photo
Editorial: Ark Creative (UK) Ltd
Design: Ark Creative (UK) Ltd

ISBN: 978-0-31909-108-1

While every care has been taken to ensure the accuracy of the route directions, the
publishers cannot accept responsibility for errors or omissions, or for changes in
details given. The countryside is not static: hedges and fences can be removed, field
boundaries can alter, stiles can be replaced by gates, footpaths can be rerouted and
changes in ownership can result in the closure or diversion of some concessionary
paths. Also, paths that are easy and pleasant for walking in fine conditions may
become slippery, muddy and difficult in wet weather, while stepping stones across
rivers and streams may become impassable.

If you find an inaccuracy in either the text or maps, please contact Trotman
Publishing at the address below.

First published in Great Britain 2011 by Crimson Publishing and reprinted with
amendments in 2019.

This edition first published 2020 by Trotman Publishing.

Trotman Publishing, 19-21D Charles Street, Bath, BA1 1HX
www.pathfinderwalks.co.uk

Printed in India by Replika Press Pvt. Ltd. 3/20

A catalogue record for this book is available from the British Library.

Front cover: Stanage Edge
Previous page: Three Shire Heads

Ordnance Survey